Robert Grieve

New Bedford Semi-Centennial Souvenir

Containing a review of the history of the city, together with accounts of

the whale fishery, the early industries, the great growth in the cotton

manufacture and the social and economic changes

Robert Grieve

New Bedford Semi-Centennial Souvenir
Containing a review of the history of the city, together with accounts of the whale fishery, the early industries, the great growth in the cotton manufacture and the social and economic changes

ISBN/EAN: 9783337324186

Printed in Europe, USA, Canada, Australia, Japan

Cover: Foto ©ninafisch / pixelio.de

More available books at **www.hansebooks.com**

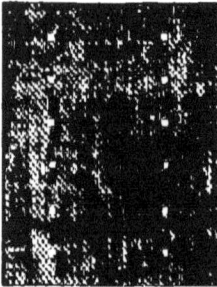

MORSE TWIST DRILL AND MACHINE CO.

NEW BEDFORD, MASS., U. S. A.

E S. TABER,
President & Treas'r.

INCORPORATED
1864

MANUFACTURERS OF

MACHINISTS' TOOLS.

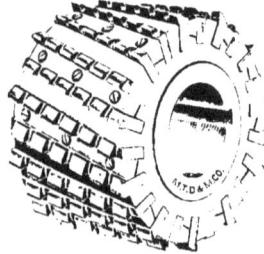

NEW BEDFORD

SEMI-CENTENNIAL SOUVENIR

CONTAINING

A Review of the History of the City

TOGETHER WITH

Accounts of the Whale Fishery, the Early Industries, the Great
Growth in the Cotton Manufacture and the Social
and Economic Changes.

ALSO

PROGRAMME OF THE SEMI-CENTENNIAL EXERCISES, LIST OF COMMITTEES,
ROUTES OF PROCESSIONS, LIST OF EXHIBITORS AT THE
INDUSTRIAL EXHIBITION, ETC.

ILLUSTRATED BY OVER 100 PHOTO-ENGRAVINGS.

EDITED BY

ROBERT GRIEVE

Author of "An Illustrated History of Pawtucket, Central Falls and Vicinity," etc.

PUBLISHED BY THE

Journal of Commerce Company

PROVIDENCE, R. I., U. S. A.

CONTENTS.

Historic and Descriptive Articles.

NEW BEDFORD
SEMI-CENTENNIAL SOUVENIR.

New Bedford, Mass.   1847 · OCTOBER - 1897.   Price 25 Cents.

Journal of Commerce Co., Publishers.

J. D. HALL, Pres. & Mgr.   GEORGE A. WILSON, Treas.
ROBERT GRIEVE, Sec.
101 SABIN ST , PROVIDENCE, R. I.

TO OUR READERS AND PATRONS.

It has not been the object of the publishers of this Souvenir of New Bedford's Semi-Centennial to present at this time an elaborate or exhaustive history of the city, but rather to depict in as popular, graphic and comprehensive a manner as the circumstances would permit, the life and growth of the community. The time at our disposal has been so limited—the work on the publication having all been done since the first of September—that no great amount of elaboration or originality has been possible in the text, and the editor has, therefore, been compelled to cull from readily accessible sources the information and facts contained in these pages. Nevertheless, we feel confident that the summaries of the various phases of the history of the city here printed will afford a fairly accurate idea to the reader, at a slight cost of time and attention, of the salient features of the story of its development, and of the influences that have made the community what it is.

The General Committee of the Semi-Centennial Celebration, on Aug. 23, voted to endorse and recognize this publication as the official souvenir of the Celebration, with the proviso that it be a creditable production. The publishers have lived up to this agreement, as the illustrations and text amply prove; but owing to a marked division of sentiment among the business men and the people of the city as to the wisdom of holding the Celebration at this time, they have not received the financial support that their own exertions, the excellence of the publication, or the importance of the occasion merited. Still, notwithstanding many discouragements, they have persevered, and with the assistance of the committee and the public-spirited men and firms, whose patronage they have received, they have succeeded in producing the present book. With diffidence, but yet with a certain amount of confidence, they present this publication to the people of New Bedford and the friends of the city, with the hope that it will aid in some small measure in still further promoting the growth and progress of the city in all essentials.

JOURNAL OF COMMERCE CO.,
PROVIDENCE, R. I.

1-W

NEW BEDFORD.

A REVIEW OF THE ORIGIN, LIFE AND GROWTH OF THE CITY.

I.

Introductory.

NEW BEDFORD cannot trace her history back to the first settlements by the white men in New England, and cannot boast of an early colonial experience. Notwithstanding this lack of an historic background, the story of the evolution of the community has in it so many incidents and changes manifesting energy and resource, that it rivals in interest the narratives of many of the most noted of the old colonial towns and cities, and exceeds in attractiveness the majority of them.

In a more perfect manner, probably, than any other American seaport, New Bedford connects the commercial era that, in its exclusive features, has passed away, with the manufacturing era that now is. These two great phases of industrial life have been manifested in her experience during the last fifty years, and she has thereby been—in a much greater degree than the majority of places in New England—an epitome of the industrial progress of the times. In these respects, because of the quick growth and rapid changes, the city has had some qualities in common with the new towns and cities of the West, which grow to large proportions in a few years.

While the city cannot claim antiquity, her citizens have been markedly distinguished for the qualities that may almost be justly called "American," namely, courage to enter new fields and engage in new enterprises, coupled with abounding vim, vigor and fertility of resource.

Starting originally as a small fishing hamlet, on the shore of a primeval forest, a few years before the revolution, the place grew vigorously for a few years. Then the war wave swept over it and almost destroyed it. Slowly it revived, and after peace came, the village increased to such a size that in 1787 it was set off from the town of Dartmouth, and became an independent town under its present name. From that time on it grew rapidly in importance, and became the greatest whaling port on the American continent. This business attained its maximum in 1857, when

New Bedford's fleet consisted of 324 vessels, manned by 10000 seamen and representing an invested capital of $12,000,000. In addition, many industries having to do with making supplies for the ships or with the manufacture of oil, were carried on in the place.

From 1857 the whale fishery began to decline in importance, so slowly at first as to be almost imperceptible. Meanwhile, however, ten years before- in 1847 the cotton manufacture had been started. Although no one then dreamed that such would be the fact, yet the event proved that this latter industry

trolling business. Indeed, the city now ranks second in the United States as a cotton manufacturing centre, and is only exceeded in this line by Fall River.

The progress and growth of New Bedford under these circumstances was phenomenal, and has not been rivalled by any Eastern city. With its main means of livelihood slowly dwindling in importance, instead of drifting into a condition of decay, as some of the old seaports have done, it sprang into a new life. Its citizens proved equal to the occasion, and turned what appeared to be a defeat into a victory. The

achievements will be that a greater impetus will be given to all worthy endeavor in the direction of progress; the young will be inspired with a desire for emulation, and the whole community will be infused with new life.

II.
The Founding and Growth of the City.

The founder of the original community, out of which the city of New Bedford ultimately developed, was Joseph Russell, who, about the middle of the last century, established himself on the shores of the Acushnet River, near the present foot of Union street. The land in the vicinity was covered with the primeval forest, and within the limits of the city of to-day there were no houses except those of the Russell family, in whose possession the territory had been for several generations.

Joseph Russell engaged in the whale fishery. At that period whales were plentiful in near-by waters, and could be readily caught with small vessels and crude appliances. The blubber was cut up and brought ashore, where a try-works had been erected to care for it and extract the oil. In this primitive way

the industry started, Joseph Russell meanwhile carrying on his farm on the hill, from which a cart path led down to the wharves and try-works. As a part of his business he began the manufacture of candles from spermaceti, and it is claimed he was the first to engage in this industry. In consequence of Mr. Russell's enterprise, a little seaside hamlet gradually came into being, and other men of industry were soon attracted. The names of some of these pioneers that have come down to us are: John Loudon, a caulker; Benjamin Taber, a boatbuilder and block-

Old Longshoremen and Ship Keepers.
Along the Wharves—Ship James Arnold and Schooner Lottie Beard.
Merrill's Wharf, Cape Verde Islands Packets.

maker; John Alden, a house carpenter; Brazilla Myrick, a ship carpenter; Elnathan Sampson, a blacksmith, and Gideon Mosher, a mechanic.

The man, however, who is credited with having given the greatest impetus to the growth of the place was Joseph Rotch, who came to the shores of the Acushnet in 1765. He was possessed of some capital, was a native of Nantucket, and had obtained some experience in the whale fishery in his native island, which was then the headquarters of that industry. He introduced better methods, and under his direction, as well as influenced by his example, the fishery was gradually extended, industry increased, and the

little hamlet became a flourishing and busy village. Until after the arrival of Joseph Rotch from Nantucket the village had no name. This fact is in itself sufficient to show of what little importance the locality then was. Soon, however, with the increase in business and population the necessity of distinguishing the place from the rest of the town became apparent, and Joseph Rotch is said to have suggested the name "Bedford," in honor of the Russell family, who bore the same family name as the English Duke of Bedford. This name was accordingly adopted, and continued in use until the incorporation of the town, when, to distinguish it from another place of the same name in the State, the word "New" was prefixed.

The village of Bedford was within the limits of the old town of Dartmouth, which was incorporated in 1664, and included the present towns of Dartmouth, Westport, Fairhaven, Acushnet, the city of New Bedford and a strip of Tiverton and Little Compton, R. I. This region had been purchased from the Indians in 1652, on behalf of the Plymouth colony, by John Cooke and Edward Winslow, for "thirty yards of cloth, eight moose skins, fifteen axes, fifteen hoes, fifteen pairs of breeches, eight blankets, two kettles, one clock, £2 in wampum, eight pair stockings, eight pair shoes, one iron pot, and ten shillings in another commodity." The deed was signed by Wamsutta, the son of Massasoit, chief of the Wampanoags, whose headquarters were near the present town of Warren, R. I., and who figures so conspicuously in the accounts of the dealings of the first colonists with the Indians. Part of this territory had been apportioned to some of the first settlers of Plymouth by the general court as early as 1639, and Capt. Miles Standish had a right to a "plantation" here. Few of the Pilgrims, however, removed to Dartmouth, but the settlers were mainly Quakers and Baptist, who were able to influence the local legislation to such an extent "that the town, as a town, never once levied or paid a tax to support a preacher or to build a house of worship, or elected a preacher who would receive any part of his support from the public treasury." This is a notable record, in view of

the fact that in the Old Colony and in Massachusetts there was a practical union between church and State, which, whatever its original justification, ultimately worked disaster and oppression. The inhabitants of the new village of Bedford were of this independent, free thinking, freedom-loving class of people, and their influence on the development of the place was marked and salutary.

From 1765 to the time of the Revolution the village grew rapidly for the times, and many people settled in the immediate vicinity. All this was changed by the war. The whale fishery was suspended; some of the merchants fitted out their vessels as privateers, and the harbor became a rendezvous for private armed vessels. Although the leading inhabitants, being Quakers, had not countenanced this, the British forces, in retaliation, made a raid on the village Sept. 5th and 6th, 1778. Major General Grey, under orders from Sir Henry Clinton, landed at Clark's Cove on the afternoon of Sept. 5th, with between four and five thousand troops, which had been brought up the bay by the British frigate, "Carysfort," and several transports. Marching up the County road to the village, the troops there burned thirty-four vessels, ten dwelling houses and about twenty-five other buildings, and on their way killed three citizens—Abraham Russell, Thomas Cook and Diah Trafford. The troops then marched to the head of the inlet, through the present town of Acushnet, and down along the east side through Fairhaven, and re-embarked on their vessels from Sconticut Neck. The value of property destroyed on this raid amounted to £99,080, about half a million dollars, which was a great sum for as poor a community as Bedford then was.

After the war the village of Bedford recovered rapidly from the great disaster of the British raid, and increased to such an extent that, by an act passed Feb. 23, 1787, it was separated from the old town of Dartmouth, and started on its career as an independent political corporation, under the name of New Bedford. Its territory then included the present towns of Fairhaven and Acushnet.

Fairhaven was incorporated as a separate town

under an act passed Feb. 22, 1812, but it had long been a considerable village. In 1860 the territory of Fairhaven was divided and the northern portion became the town of Acushnet, where a village had existed by that name at the "Head of the River," half a century before New Bedford was founded. Oxford Village, on the east side of the river, just before and after the Revolution, rivaled Bedford in size and importance. The village of Bellville, on the west side, between Bedford and Acushnet, was likewise, at the same period, about the same size. Thus, there were five villages on the Acushnet River—Bedford, Fairhaven, Oxford, Acushnet and Bellville—all apparently with an equal chance in the race for supremacy. Bedford, however, proved to be the most favorably situated, and after the Revolution, steadily forged ahead. One circumstance that probably first gave Bedford village an advantage over its rivals was the fact that Joseph Rotch was unable to buy land on the water front in Fairhaven, and was consequently obliged to content himself with the ten acre lot he bought from Joseph Russell in 1765, on which he located, and thus all his capital and enterprise were centered in Bedford. This circumstance, combined with better natural opportunities, made Bedford the central place, and ultimately resulted in her becoming the metropolis of the region.

The leading merchant in New Bedford at the beginning of the century was William Rotch, the son of Joseph Rotch. He had remained in Nantucket when his father located on the shores of the Acushnet in 1765; from 1785 to 1793 he carried on his business at Dunkirk, France; but in 1795 he came to New Bedford. His son, William Rotch, Jr., continued the family business, and his son-in-law, Samuel Rodman, was also a whaling merchant. Among the conspicuous names in this line during the active period of the whale fishery, which followed in the next half century, were the Russells, the Howlands, the Hathaways, the Tuckers, many of whom amassed great wealth.

The growth of New Bedford after the revolution is well illustrated by the statistics of the shipping in the vicinity in 1803. The total tonnage was 19,146, and the number of vessels were 59, all belonging in the town of New Bedford except four—two of which were owned in Westport and two in Dartmouth. At that date Fairhaven was included in New Bedford. Of the total number of vessels, 20 ships and 8 brigs belonged in the village of New Bedford, and 12 ships and 9 brigs in Fairhaven. Of these, about 20 vessels were engaged in whaling and thirty as merchantmen or packets. New Bedford had the larger number of whaling craft, but Fairhaven was the port of the majority of the freighting vessels. Thus, both sides of the river were growing together at nearly an equal rate. After the division into two towns, New Bedford was but little larger than Fairhaven, and in 1820 the population, respectively, was: New Bedford, 3,047; Fairhaven, 2,733.

The war of 1812 and the embargoes antecedent thereto crippled the commerce and fishery of the port, so that at times many vessels were laid up at the wharves inactive; but with the close of the war a revival set in, which resulted in a constant and healthful growth. This growth was greatly accelerated between 1820 and 1830, owing to the noticeable increase in the demand for oil, resulting from the development of manufactures throughout New England, as a consequence of the introduction of the power loom, which rendered possible the rapid extension of the cotton and woolen industries. From 1830 until 1860 the population increased at the rate of about 5,000 each decade. For the next decade it remained stationary in fact, decreased slightly but beginning with the erection of the fourth mill of the Wamsutta corporation in 1868, there has been a constant increase at very much more than the old rate, and since 1880, with the multiplication of the cotton mills, the population has more than doubled.

In 1847 the town of New Bedford was incorporated as a city, and on April 28 of the same year the first municipal government was inaugurated.

The first mayor was Abraham Howland, who served four years 1847-51. His successors in the office have been: William J. Rotch, 1852; Rodney French, 1853-54; George Howland, Jr., 1855-56; George H. Dunbar, 1857-58; Willard Nye, 1859; Isaac C. Taber, 1860-61, and to Sept. 29, 1862; George Howland, Jr.,

1862 from Sept. 20, and 1863-65; John H. Perry, 1866-67; Andrew G. Pierce, 1868-69; George B. Richmond, 1870-72; George H. Dunbar, 1873; George B. Richmond, 1874; Abraham H. Howland, Jr., 1875-76; Manson Borden, 1877; George B. Richmond, 1878; William T. Soule, 1879-80; George Wilson, 1881-84; Morgan Rotch, 1885-88; Walter Clifford, 1889-90; Charles S. Ashley, 1891-92; Jethro C. Brock, 1893; Stephen A. Brownell, 1894; David L. Parker, 1895-96; Charles S. Ashley, 1897.

III.
Origin, Progress and Decay of the Whale Fishery.

For the first hundred years of her history, the life of New Bedford depended upon and centered around the whale fishery. Her citizens brought this hazardous real origin on the island of Nantucket. At first the whales were caught near the shores by primitive methods, and the "Off Shore" whaling continued to be followed until about the middle of the last century. As the whales became scarce or more timid, vessels were fitted out to pursue them to more distant waters, but the blubber was brought home and the oil extracted in try works on shore. Larger vessels were built and more extended voyages made, as the fishermen gained in experience, until the Nantucket sailors had penetrated every sea. The island became the home of the whale fishery, and in 1775, 150 whalers sailed from the port, manned by 2,500 seamen. The War of the Revolution practically wiped out the business, but just previous to the war of 1812, there were 40 ships from the island engaged in the fishery,

and could only be found in distant seas, so that a whaling voyage which, in the early times, had been an undertaking of a few days or weeks, finally consumed months or years. The staunch ships of New Bedford penetrated into every ocean. They went into the ice fields of the north; they rounded Cape Horn and the Cape of Good Hope, into the Pacific and Indian Oceans; they sailed into far southern latitudes, and found their way into every remote region of the globe.

Since the beginning of the village many of the vessels hailing from the port have been built here. The first ship built was the "Dartmouth," launched in 1767. She belonged to Francis Rotch, son of Joseph, and her first voyage was to London, Eng., with a cargo of whale oil. She was one of the vessels from which the tea was thrown overboard in Boston harbor in

New Bedford, with an average of a whaleship arriving every day in the year, was a busy seaport, whose life and character can hardly be realized to-day unless aided by an imagination instructed by the recitals of some of the old sailors or residents of that period.

During the War of the Rebellion, the whaling interest suffered severely. The "Alabama" burned many whaling vessels in 1862, near the Azores, and other rebel cruisers added to the destruction at other times and places. The "Shenandoah," in June, 1865, captured in Behring Straits 27 whaling vessels, burning 24 of them, and of these 17 belonged in New Bedford. The loss to New Bedford was about a million and a half of dollars. A great disaster overtook the whaling fleet September, 1871, "when in a single day 33 ships were abandoned in the Arctic Ocean, hopelessly crushed or environed in the ice."

VIEW OF NEW BEDFORD, LOOKING SOUTHWARD, FROM TOP OF ODD FELLOWS BUILDING.
With Palmer's Island and Fairhaven in the Background

1773. Her cargo consisted of 114 chests, or about one-third of the entire amount that the "Boston Tea Party" destroyed. The ship "Bedford," the property of Joseph Rotch, was the first American vessel to display the Stars and Stripes in Great Britain. She arrived in London, Feb. 23, 1783, the day of the signing of the preliminary treaty of peace, with a cargo of 587 barrels of oil.

New Bedford, with her admirable advantages as a port a lengthy water front, deep water up to the wharves, and a commodious harbor, easily accessible at all conditions of wind and tide ultimately absorbed nearly all the whaling business on the Atlantic seaboard, until in 1857 her fleet consisted of 324 vessels, worth more than $12,000,000 and requiring the service of over 10,000 seamen. In the decade from 1850 to 1860 the business was at its height, and

Of these vessels, 22 belonged in New Bedford, the loss on which, exclusive of oil and bone, was $1,000,-000. In 1876, 12 New Bedford ships were abandoned in the Arctic, entailing a loss of 50 lives and $600,000 worth of property. August 3, 1888, five whalers were lost in a gale off Point Barrow in the Arctic Ocean, three of them being New Bedford ships, the loss on which was about $500,000. The most recent disaster was the loss of the steam whaling bark, "Navarch," in the ice, 120 miles northeast of Point Barrow, together with 35 of her crew, on July 20, 1897.

About the year 1857 the whale fishery began to decline, but New Bedford has always continued to be the chief port. During the last fifteen or twenty years a considerable number of the New Bedford vessels, composing the North Pacific fleet, have been transferred to San Francisco, and that port now rivals New Bedford. January 1, 1897, the New Bedford whaling fleet consisted of 19 ships and barks, one brig and 12 schooners, of a tonnage of 6,410, while at the same date San Francisco had 21 steamers and barks and one schooner, of an aggregate tonnage of 6,498.

The constant and gradual decline of the whale fishery is due to two main causes, namely, the increasing scarcity of whales from year to year, necessitating voyages into more remote seas at a largely increased cost, and the discovery of petroleum, the use of which supplanted whale oil for many purposes. The cost of securing whale oil was thus increased, while its price in the market was lowered, with the necessary result that capital found it unprofitable to continue in the whale fishery. This movement was

STEAMSHIP WILLIAM BAYLIES,
Wintering in Arctic Ocean, Mouth of the Mackenzie River, 1

checked by a fortunate rise in the price of whalebone, which increased in market value seven or eight times its former figures. The price of sperm oil per gallon in 1855 was $1.77, and of whale oil 71 cents. In 1857 sperm oil brought $1.28, and from that time until 1877, although it fluctuated considerably, it did not fall below the dollar limit until 1878, when it averaged about 90 cents. Since then it has steadily declined, and during 1896 the average price was 40 cents. Whale oil has fluctuated in value very much less, as it averaged 35 cents a gallon in 1896. The price of whalebone in 1835 was 42 cents a pound; in 1857, 97 cents; in 1875, $1.12, while in 1896 its average price was $3.95.

The constant improvements in the manufacture of mineral and vegetable oils during the last quarter of a century have resulted in the production of lubricating oils that take the place of sperm at a very much

less cost. They do not wholly supplant sperm, but they have deposed it from its old place of sole prominence as a lubricator, a place it will never again fill. At the same time there will always be a considerable demand for it, and the whale fishery is not likely to wholly die out so long as a limited market remains for the oil, and there is a great demand for whalebone at the large prices that now prevail.

In the common life of New England, New Bedford has always cut a much larger figure and has been much more widely known than other places of equal population and business. The young men from the remote farms, the rugged hillsides, the inland towns or cities, moved by a desire to see something of the world and its wonders, made their way to the wharves of the whaling city, and from thence set forth on their quest after adventure and fortune. That they did not always realize either, in the manner or in the degree that fancy led them to expect, did not prevent others from following in their footsteps. But the experiences they did achieve, although perhaps somewhat severe to most of those who ventured, still had elements of romance, especially when viewed, seated in a pleasant home, through the haze of memory. Scarcely a place in the limits of the Atlantic seaboard but furnished, one or two generations ago, some adventurous son, who either went by consent or ran away to New Bedford and shipped on a whaler. In how many books of biography and newspaper obituaries are accounts even now found of men who thus began life by shipping from the old whaling port? By how many cosy firesides, in lonely farm houses, in village homes, in city dwellings, have the seafaring adventures of friends and relatives been discussed, and with what all absorbed interest have the hearers followed the details of the narrative, especially if the narrator had himself been a participant, and possessed the sailor's usual gift of "spinning a yarn?"

Although New Bedford is shorn of her old glory as a port, her harbor presents many picturesque reminders of the past in the shape of old whaling ships, lying dismantled in the docks. Then, too, occasionally the din of the hammers of the ship carpenter and the caulker is heard on her wharves, when one of her small remaining fleet is being prepared for sea. But she has more than made up for her losses by the phenomenal growth of her manufactures; her water front is dotted with vessels of a coastwise com-

Ship South America.   Ship Archer.

*THE STONE FLEET, WHICH SAILED FROM NEW BEDFORD NOV. 16, 1861.

... ... TOGRAPH BY S. FRANK & CO., NOW IN POSSESSION OF WILLIAM BAYLIES   COPYRIGHTED BY BEN ...

merce bringing supplies to her manufacturers, and she has taken a front rank as a textile manufacturing city, in this way sustaining her reputation as a leader in whatever she undertakes.

* THE STONE FLEET.—So many whalers were obliged to tie up to the wharves at the beginning of the civil war, that when the Government wished to secure a number of vessels for the purpose of sinking them, loaded with stone, at the entrances to Southern harbors, the New Bedford merchants were willing to dispose of many of their ships at almost any price. Of the "Stone Fleet," of 45 vessels, that was used in this manner to blockade Southern ports, 24 were New Bedford crafts. The illustration of these vessels, shown on this page, was made from an old engraving, and represents the fleet in New Bedford lower harbor on Nov. 16, 1861, on the eve of sailing. About 7,500 tons of stone were carried out by them from New Bedford, and most of them were sunk in the harbor of Charlestown, S. C., and effectively blockaded that port at first. In time, it is said, however, the effect was a decided blessing to Charlestown, as the immense mass of stone formed a jetty, which directed the currents in such a manner as to form a much deeper and better channel than formerly. The list of vessels, and the order in which they appear in the engraving, beginning at the left, is as follows:

Bark "Garland," Capt. Rodney French, 243 tons, 190 tons stone; ship "Maria Theresa," Capt. T. S. Bailey, 330 tons, 320 tons stone; revenue cutter "Varina," Capt. Sands; bark "American," Capt. W. A. Beard, 320 tons, 300 tons stone; pilot boats "Rescue" and "Richmond;" ship "Rebecca Simms," Capt. J. F. Willis, 400 tons, 425 tons stone; bark "Harvest," Capt. W. W. Taylor, 314 tons, 400 tons stone; bark "Leonidas," Capt. J. Howland, 231 tons, 200 tons stone; bark "Amazon," Capt. J. S. Swift, 318 tons, 328 tons stone; ship "South America," Capt. David G. Chadwick, 646 tons, 550 tons stone; pilot boat "Effort;" bark "Cossack," Capt. Childs, 250 tons, 250 tons stone; ship "Archer," Capt. Worth, 321 tons, 280 tons stone; pilot boat "Vision;" ship "Courier," Capt. Shubael F. Brayton, 381 tons, 350 tons stone; bark "Francis Henrietta," Capt. Michael Cumisky, 407 tons, 381 tons stone; ship "Potomac," Capt. Brown, 356 tons, 350 tons stone; ship "Kensington," Capt. B. F. Tilton, 357 tons, 350 tons stone; bark "Herald," Capt. A. H. Gifford, 274 tons, 240 tons stone; ship "L. C. Richmond," Capt. Malloy, 341 tons, 300 tons stone.

A second fleet of seven vessels sailed from New Bedford, Dec. 9, 1861, consisting of the following vessels: Ships "America," Capt. Henry B. Chase; "William Lee," Capt. Horace A. Lake; barks "India," Capt. Avery F. Parker; "Mechanic," Capt. Archibald Baker, Jr.; "Valparaiso," Capt. William Wood; "Margaret Scott," Capt. Henry F. Tobey; "Majestic," Capt. Joseph Dimmick.

2-W

IV.

Social and Economic Conditions — The Changes of the Years.

The phases of life that have been presented in the experience of New Bedford have been so varied, that the social and human sides of her history have thereby many more points of interest than is usually the case with a small community situated away from the great main currents of the world's affairs. This was at first owing to the unique nature of the calling her people have depended on for their livelihood, which attracted men from all parts of the country and brought in men of all nations; and, second, its continuance is due to the fact that the rise of manufacturing by introducing again people of many nationalities has intermixed and superimposed other influences on the existing social peculiarities.

"Going down to the sea in ships" brought to her inhabitants a wide knowledge of other countries and peoples, and contributed to make them broader in view, more tolerant in judgment and to give them a certain amount of culture. These characteristics were by no means at the same time found in the same degree in less favored communities. That this is not a fanciful assumption is borne out by the facts. The high character of many of her leading merchants and of her common citizens is well exhibited by the institutions they created, and by their life and works in many lines.

The early inhabitants of New Bedford were Quakers. The Russells, the Rotchs, most of the leading merchants and many of the mechanics and permanent citizens were of this persuasion. The influence of the sect for a long time dominated the community; and the high standard of living enjoined, the austere manners inculcated, and the clear and wholesome views of doctrine taught, all contributed to give a

PUBLIC LIBRARY AND ODD FELLOWS BUILDING.

no ... that a very large number of fugitive slaves, aided by many of our most wealthy and respectable citizens, have left for Canada and parts unknown, and that men are in the way of departure. The utmost sympathy and liberality prevails ward the class of our citizens."

Hon. Frederick Douglas, the great anti-slavery orator, and the most eminent man the colored race has yet produced in this country, found refuge in New Bedford, where he worked as a mechanic, and laid the foundations of the education that afterwards enabled him to accomplish so much for his people.

A contrast to the

healthful tone to the life of the community, while the crudities and peculiarities in some particulars of the Friends were overcome by the wider experience of life brought to the community by commerce and the influx of new life.

The Quakers opposed slavery, they freed their own slaves about the time of the revolution, and the New Bedford Friends were both theoretically and practically abolitionists in the middle years of the century, when they rescued many fugitive negroes and helped them to liberty by the clandestine means known by the name of the Underground Railroad. Daniel Ricketson says: "In the early years of the century there was hardly a house in the place which had not given shelter and succor to a fugitive slave." The Fugitive Slave law passed in 185 evidently had few supporters in New Bedford, as the following paragraph from the Mercury of April, 1851, indicates:

events and sentiments just recorded is presented by the scenes of dissipation that, during this same period, were happening in the lower part of the town. Like all seaports it had its dens of iniquity, and frequently outrages occurred. Incited by a murder which had been committed in the neighborhood, a mob of citizens, in August, 1826, burned a number

READING ROOM, PUBLIC LIBRARY.

of houses tenanted by abandoned characters, at a locality known as "Hard Dig," on Kempton street, a little west of the present base ball park. The next night the mob burned "The Ark," an old whaler which was beached on the spot where Charles S. Paisler's brick building now stands on North Water street. A house had been built on the hull of the vessel, and it was a low resort of the worst possible character.

A second "Ark" was soon after built, also on the hull of a whaler, and was located in the same neighborhood as the first had been. "It was occupied by the worst classes, and was the abode of debauchery and evil doing. Citizens were in daily fear, not only of their property but of their lives. Any attempt to

posed persons. Nor was this confined to Howland street for South Water street and other intersecting streets partook of the generally bad reputation. They abounded in dance halls, saloons, gambling dens and brothels. When our ships came in from their long voyages these abodes of iniquity were in high carnival, fights and brawls were of frequent occurrence, and it was dangerous to pass through this section after nightfall. It was no uncommon occurrence for persons to be knocked down and robbed. Matters grew steadily worse and more uncontrollable, when a climax was reached in a murder." The rioters destroyed two houses by fire on that occasion, and effectually frightened the degraded denizens of the neighborhood.

COUNTY STREET, THE MAIN RESIDENCE AVENUE.

banish the scourge failed, and it soon became evident that law was held in effectual defiance." When affairs had reached this pass, an organized band of disguised citizens took the matter up and burned the second "Ark" Aug. 27, 1829. Leading citizens, in order to prevent any further destruction of property by mob violence, organized a vigilance committee, which finally became the "Protecting Society," now the oldest part of the fire department.

The Howland street riot occurred on the evening of April 19, 1856, and was similar in its intent and purpose to the "Ark" riots of 1826 and 1829. A murder had been committed in the south part of the city on Howland street. This neighborhood in the years previous, and especially at the time of the riot "was a noted resort for drunken sailors and evil dis-

The life of the town in those days necessarily revolved around the whaling interest. The arrival of a whaler was always an interesting event. By a system of signals, the approach of an incoming ship was ascertained before it entered the bay. Boats immediately put out to meet the vessel, crowded with boarding house keepers, ship agents and other interested parties. On the wharf a crowd had collected by this time, as from the lookouts it had been definitely learned who the vessel belonged to, and its landing place therefore ascertained. Soon the ship was brought into the dock, tied up, and immediately the work of unloading the oil and stripping the vessel of her sails and outfit began. Meanwhile the sailors were the object of much solicitude to the various boarding house keepers, especially if the voyage had

YOUNG MEN'S CHRISTIAN ASSOCIATION BUILDING.

been a successful one. In the palmy days of the fishery their revenues were large, as they not only boarded and lodged the seamen, but advanced money to them on their shares, and acted as shipping agents. The sharp practices of which this class were guilty gained for them the name of "sharkers" or "land sharks," conveying the idea, which was unfortunately too often true, that the poor sailor was shown as little mercy by many of them on land as he would be by the "tiger of the sea" if at his mercy in the water. The manner of conducting a whaling voyage was to give each participant a certain lay or share in the oil or bone obtained, in proportion to their rank or value of service. In addition to the scarcity of whales and the introduction of petroleum, other causes contributed to the decline of the business. Some of these are recounted as follows by George F. Tucker, in his article on New Bedford, in the *New England Magazine* for September, 1890:

"Another cause of the decline was the deterioration of the seamen. The foremast hand of fifty years ago was a farmer's boy. He carried homespun garments, and was rarely the debtor of the ship. He was ambitious to advance, and, if he never became a master, he was reasonably sure of becoming an officer. In later years an unre-

liable element dominated the forecastle. There was hardly a sailor who was not a debtor of the ship for his outfit; improvident and indifferent, he entered upon his labors with little of the zeal of his hardy predecessor."

The American sailors, not finding the business profitable, sought other fields and occupations, and the crews of the whalers were either recruited from the class Mr. Tucker refers to, or were composed of men of other nationalities, content with small returns. The effect of all this was to bring about new social and industrial conditions. Many of the new sailors were men of Portuguese descent, natives of the Azores, or Western Islands. They began to ship as sailors in the prosperous days of the fishery, and the ships still in commission are manned largely by them. At present the people of this nationality form a considerable proportion of the population, and reside chiefly on South Water street and its neighborhood.

While all these changes were taking place, the fundamental character of the people was finding expression in the establishing of schools and institutions that aided materially in social growth. There were no public schools, except for the poor, until 1821, when action was taken that resulted in an excellent school system that was developed to a great degree of efficiency as the years passed. The High School was first opened June 11, 1827, and the present fine edifice was erected in 1876. The Friends' Academy, founded by William Rotch, dates from 1810, has always been an excellent institution, and is now a day school for teaching boys and girls ancient and modern languages, mathematics, and natural and moral sci-

ence. The Swain Free School, started Oct. 25, 1882, in the Swain family mansion, bequeathed for that purpose by William W. Swain, is an excellent institution for the teaching of the classics, history and literature.

The "Aimwell" is an excellent private school, established in 1861, by Mrs. D. P. Knight. It is now conducted in the Young Men's Christian Association building, by Miss Mary R. Hinckley, who was a faithful and capable teacher in the public schools for many years. The school is easily accessible from every direction, and the surroundings, both within and without the building, are such as to directly aid in the moral and mental development of the pupils.

One of the first organizations in the United States to engage scholarly and eminent men to lecture on literary and scientific subjects, was the New Bedford Lyceum, founded in 1828, and it continued to do so until the decadence of lyceum lecturing.

The chief enterprise, however, that manifested the inclination and desire of the people of New Bedford for intellectual culture, was the establishing of the Free Public Library, by a city ordinance passed July 20, 1852. It was first opened to the public on March 3, 1853, and was one of the first free public libraries in the United States. The library building was finished in 1857, and a large addition was completed and opened in 1886. From the opening of the library Robert C. Ingraham has been librarian. To his skill as an organizer and administrator, his acquirements as a scholar, and his thorough and comprehensive knowledge of the books in his care, much of the credit of the effectiveness of the library is due. The library has exercised a very potent influence on the life of the city, and has been, in the best sense, a dispenser of light, and a source of mental and moral growth.

Organizations for benevolent and charitable work are numerous in New Bedford. One of the earliest and best known of these is the New Bedford Port Society established in 1830, which maintains a Bethel and a Seamen's Home on Second street. The New Bedford Ladies' City Mission originated in 1846 as a tract society, and for more than thirty years has maintained a mission at the South End on South Water street.

The Union for Good Works was incorporated in 1872 for the promotion of religious, educational and charitable purposes, and had commodious quarters in the Hicks Building on Purchase street, comprising a

reading room with a good library, and an amusement room with suitable appliances for many kinds of games, until 1895, when it moved into a beautiful new building of its own on Market street, opposite the City Hall. The rooms here contain all the old time attractions and others in addition, and the association is also engaged in effective charitable work. The Orphan's Home, corner of Cove street and French avenue, at the southern extremity of the city, was established in 1843, and is supported by contributions and the income of invested funds. The Association for the Relief of Aged Women formed in 1866 for the purpose of affording "assistance and relief to respectable, aged American women," distributes several thousand dollars annually. The city has two excellent hospitals, St. Luke's on Fourth street, estab-

VIEW ON PURCHASE STREET.

lished in 1884; and St. Joseph's on Pleasant street, started in 1872. They are both admirably conducted and the latter is under the control of the Sisters of Mercy.

The Young Men's Christian Association of New Bedford was first organized in 1851, but soon lapsed for lack of interest. It was revived in 1867, and since then has had a constant and prosperous existence. The present beautiful building of the association, corner of William and Sixth streets, was erected in 1890.

The oldest church in New Bedford is the First Congregational, originally an orthodox society that worshipped at Acushnet, but which became Unitarian early in the century. The present substantial stone edifice on Union street, near County, was erected in 1838. Among the preachers of this church have been several eminent men. Dr. Samuel West was the minister from 1760 to 1803, and in the latter years of his pastorate the church was removed to New Bedford. Orville Dewey was the minister from 1823 to 1834. Ralph Waldo Emerson supplied the pulpit for six months during Dr. Dewey's pastorate. John Weiss was the preacher from 1847 to 1858. William J. Potter was the minister from 1859 until his death a few years ago. He was a man of great intellectual powers, a true preacher of righteousness and truth, and his influence and example on the community was marked and wholesome. The North Congregational Church, which is an orthodox body, is an offshoot of the First Church, and the present stone edifice on Purchase street was erected in 1836. The Trinitarian Church is the child of the North Congregational, and its fine edifice on Fourth street was erected in 1891. The pastor of this church is Matthew C. Julien, an unusually powerful and eloquent preacher. The North Christian church, a large wooden building with pillars in front,

their ideas, manners and modes of life differed in many particulars. These observations apply particularly to the English, Scotch and Irish immigrants, who formed the bulk of the original factory population. But if the points of difference between them and the natives were great, how much greater were they in the case of the French Canadians and other peoples that speak a foreign language, who coming in at a later period than the first European immigrants had little in common either with them or with the native inhabitants.

Under such conditions it was difficult for the various elements of the population to understand each other. Time and experience together has brought a measure of mutual comprehension, and allayed race and national prejudices. The freedom of political intercourse has also contributed to break down the barriers, and the new inhabitants have taken hold eagerly and hopefully in the struggles of our "fierce (but free) Democracy." They have thereby been educated, and have become good citizens, the equals of the old guard.

WAMSUTTA MILLS.

and a tall spire, is situated on Purchase street; it was erected in 1833, and is known as the "White House" from its color. One of the handsomest edifices in the city is Grace church, Episcopal, on County street, which was dedicated in 1881. The Methodists have eight churches, the Baptists have four, the Catholics have five—two English speaking, two French and a Portuguese church. There are over thirty places of public worship in the city. The first building for worship was the Friends' Meeting house, built in 1785, which gave place to the present brick edifice, erected in 1829.

The new population brought in by the increase of the cotton industry after 1870, found all these institutions and advantages ready to hand, and many made use of them. They used the library, joined the societies, united with the churches, and their children attended the schools. But still the new comers formed a class apart from the old inhabitants. Although the majority of them were of the same race and had inherited the same body of tradition as the city's people, they were natives of other countries and

The result of the fraternizing that has by this means been brought about has been the dwindling of old prejudices, and a greater tendency to accept each man for his "sense and worth" and not for his ancestry, his wealth or his connections.

While in a large way this growth in understanding each other is an undeniable fact, yet the factory people have been to many of the old inhabitant an alien race, of whose life and struggles they knew as little as they did of those of the inhabitants of some far off country, for whom their sympathy might occasionally be excited by an act of oppression or a tale of wrong. In reality it was difficult for the well housed, cultured natives with their manifold advantages to realize that the uncouth, poorly dressed and ignorant factory hands were human beings of like passions and aspirations with themselves, and that the differences were more superficial and apparent than real. This lesson has, however, been learned in the school of experience where so many that were first are now last and those that were last are first.

In our country it has been said "there are only three generations from shirt sleeves to shirt sleeves." The experiences of this community for the past quarter of a century gives color to this generalization, for the direction of the industrial energies has, with the growth of the city, passed in many instances into new hands. Many who were rich are now poor, and some who were poor are now rich. These results were accidental in numerous instances, poor investments being the cause in the one direction, and the rise in the value of land the means in the other. Yet thereby new social combinations have been evolved. New Bedford, on account of her varied industrial experiences, has exhibited more social flux and reflux than most contemporary communities. The end is not yet; but the changes that have taken place have made for progress, and for a social structure adapted to the new conditions.

V.

Manufacturing, Its Beginning, Growth and Development.

While the whale fishery for the first hundred years of her history was the main source of New Bedford's wealth, yet during this period progress was made in

the first manufacturer, converting the blubber of the whales his little vessels had caught, into oil in his try works on shore. Joseph Russell also manufactured candles from spermaceti previous to the revolution, in a building which stood near the corner of Centre and Front streets, employing as superintendent a Capt. Chafee, at the then enormous salary of $500.00 per annum. All the principal whaling merchants had their oil and candle factories. William Rotch & Son are said to have built the old "Marsh Candle Works," which occupied the site on which the gas works now stand, and where Francis Rotch and Charles W. Morgan subsequently carried on the manufacture. The factory of Samuel Rodman was on the corner of Water and Rodman streets. Humphrey Hathaway and Isaac Howland, Jr., had factories on School street. John James Howland built candle works at the corner of Second and Middle streets, which were in operation as early as 1815. The build-

POTOMSKA MILLS.

developing various manufactures. The whale fishery necessarily attracted certain industries. Ships, boats and supplies were required, and the village which grew up around the wharves of Joseph Russell and Joseph Rotch was formed of mechanics and dealers who catered to these demands. Consequently the first inhabitants were shipbuilders, riggers, sailmakers, carpenters, blacksmiths, painters, boatbuilders, caulkers, coopers, blockmakers, rope and chainmakers, etc., and store keepers dealing in ship chandlery and supplies. Thus from the very beginning there was a great diversity of industry, - unusual for a community of its size, - the effect of which was to produce a readiness of resource and an adaptability among the inhabitants that enabled them and their descendants in after times, when necessity demanded, to turn their energies readily into other channels.

The manufacture and refining of oil was the first industry carried on in an organized way, in factories, and has continued to the present one of the most important. The founder of the city was in reality

ing, a substantial two story stone structure is still standing. For many years it was utilized as a soap factory by Otis Sisson and others, and is still the scene of that industry, under the management of Brett & Simpson. George Hussey and James Henry Howland established the factory at the Smoking Rocks, soon after the elder Mr. Howland had started his factory on Middle street. William W. Swain built a factory on the north side of Middle street. Andrew Robeson built a factory on Ray street, which subsequently came into the possession of Edward Mott Robinson. George Howland had a factory on Howland's wharf and William T. Russell engaged in the manufacture on Third street. Charles W. Morgan carried on oil works on South Water street. One of the older factories was on First street, and was established by David Coffin.

As the whaling business increased during the first quarter of the century the manufacture of oil and candles became specialized, and a number of factories were erected in what is now the central and south parts of the city by firms which devoted their entire attention to this business. The largest oil refiner at the time when the whale fishery was at its height, was Samuel Leonard, who established the factory on Leonard street, east of Water street. Other

factory on Prospect street, now conducted by George S. Homer. A number of the old factories still exist in a dismantled condition, but the majority of them have been converted to other uses.

The refining and distillation of coal oil was begun

VIEW OF THE ACUSHNET AND HATHAWAY MILLS FROM THE WATER FRONT.

refiners who carried on large businesses were Nehemiah Leonard, a brother of Samuel; Sydney Howland; George T. Baker, who established the factories now carried on by George Delanos' Sons, and W. A. Robinson & Co.; Cornelius Grinnell, who had a factory

about the year 1857, by the New Bedford Coal Oil Co., the works of Joseph Ricketson being utilized for the purpose, and the claim has been made that petroleum was first successfully refined in this establishment in 1860, by Weston Howland, the secretary of the

the refining of sperm and whale oil. These are George Delanos' Sons, W. A. Robinson & Co., George S. Homer, oil and candles, and William F. Nye, maker of sewing machine and watch and clock oils.

A rope walk was in operation in the village previous to the revolution, but was burned by the British soldiers in 1778. Probably another took its place after the war. The New Bedford Cordage Co., which has remained until the present one of the leading industries, was established in 1842. Its plant now covers four acres in the west part of the city and employes about 250 hands.

The Morse Twist Drill & Machine Co. is one of the largest industries, and to it belongs the credit of founding and developing the manufacture of the well known "Morse Twist Drill."

Mr. S. A. Morse, the inventor of the "Morse Patent Straight-Lip Increase Twist Drill," in 1864, so interested some few of the New Bedford business men in his patents, that they organized a company for the purpose of manufacturing under these patents. A start was made with a capital stock of $30,000, in a modest two-story wooden building, 30 x 60. From year to year the business has steadily increased, and additions have been required to both capital and plant, until to-day, after a lapse of thirty-three years, the corporation has a capital stock of $600,000, and its buildings cover nearly a square.

The main building is of brick, three stories in height, 390 x 35, while the total floor area of all the buildings is nearly two acres. About 350 people are employed. The reputation of the "Morse Drills" has not been confined to the United States, but a large export trade has been built up, and the goods go all over the world, being distributed through export merchants in this country, or through the agencies maintained in England, France, Germany and Austria. Mr. Edward S. Taber is president and treasurer, to which offices he was elected in 1868.

The carriage manufacture was begun in New Bedford during the first quarter of the century. Among the pioneers of the industry were Ayres R. Marsh and Joseph Brownell, the father of J. Augustus Brownell, of the present firm of Brownell, Ashley & Co. George L.

3-11

NEW BEDFORD MANUFACTURING CO., Foot of Hillman St.

HOWLAND MILLS CO., South End

ROTCH SPINNING CO., South End.

Brownell started in business in the early forties. Other leading industries are the New Bedford Copper Co., incorporated in 1860, and at present employing 100 hands; the Pairpoint Manufacturing Co., silver plated ware and glass, established in 1880, but which is also the owner of the Mount Washington

VI.
Growth of the Cotton Manufacture.
The Wamsutta Mills.

In the middle years of the century, when the whaling business was at its height, Thomas Bennett,

MILL OF THE PIERCE MANUFACTURING CO.

Glass Works, started in 1869, the combined plants now employing 600 hands; Taber Art Co., dating from 1847, employing about 250 hands; New Bedford Iron Foundry established in 1847; Hathaway Soule & Harrington, shoe manufacturers, established in 1865, and employing at present 300 hands.

Jr., a young man, a native of Fairhaven, who had had some experience in a cotton mill in the South, conceived the idea of establishing a cotton factory on his own account. He came to New Bedford in an endeavor to raise capital, and ultimately succeeded, mainly through the assistance of Joseph Grinnell, in

MILL OF THE BRISTOL MANUFACTURING CO.

The diversified character of the city's industries can be realized by the enumeration of some of the principal lines of work. Besides those mentioned there are boiler works, brass foundries, a rocket manufactory, candle and soap factories, picture frame shops, planing mills, boatbuilding yards, and other shops and industries too numerous to mention in detail.

organizing a company. The task of getting the people of New Bedford interested in the enterprise was a difficult one, as a manufacturing enterprise of this description was entirely new to them, and they preferred to continue along the lines to which they were accustomed. Most of the subscriptions to the stock were obtained by Edward L. Baker. Nearly all the leading men took shares, but in small amounts. The principal stockholders were Gideon Howland, Sylvia Ann Howland, Thomas Mandell, Ward M. Parker, Thomas Mandell, Joseph Delano and Pardon Tillinghast.

The first mill of the Wamsutta Corporation, a stone structure 212 by 70 feet, was commenced in 1847 and

MILLS OF THE COLUMBIA SPINNING CO.

David R. Greene, Latham Cross, and Grinnell, Minturn & Co., of New York. The Massachusetts legislature granted a charter to the new corporation started the next year. A second mill, a little larger than the first, was erected in 1854. and a third, which was a duplicate of the second, was built in 1860.

a mill 570 feet long 95 feet wide and three stories in height was put up, and in 1893, the last of the series, No. 7, which is however only a weaving mill and contains no preparatory machinery, was built. These seven mills are in one group on the shore of the Acush-

consequently, justly be called the father of the cotton manufacture in New Bedford. Under Mr. Bennett's management nothing but sheetings were manufactured, and they held the first place in the market and commanded the highest price. Since that time,

THE ONEKO WOOLEN MILL.

net River, at the north part of the city, and at the present time contain 230,000 spindles, 4,450 looms, and give employment to 2,100 persons. The present capital is $3,000,000. The products manufactured are fine and fancy cottons, sheetings and yarn.

From 1847 to 1874 Thomas Bennett, Jr., was the active manager of the Wamsutta Mills, first as superintendent and then as superintendent and agent. He

while the Wamsutta sheetings are still standard goods, in response to the demands of the period, cambrics, lawns, and fancy cottons have been made in great variety.

Mr. Bennett was succeeded as superintendent and agent in 1874 by Edward Kilburn, who held the position until 1887. Then for a few months Edward R. Milliken filled the office; January, 1888, William J.

The cotton manufacture was a side issue industrially. The factory community was composed of an alien people and the factory settlement was in fact a place apart from the main portion of the city. Situated at the north end, remote from the business centre, its existence was hardly known to many of the inhabitants. With the erection of the fourth mill in 1868, a new era dawned. The business community and the capitalists began to turn from the whale fishery, which had by that time experienced crushing blows from the competition of petroleum and the disasters of the war, and began to cast about for new avenues into which to direct their capital. After seeking investments elsewhere, the example of the success that the Wamsutta Mills had made, finally led to the organiza-

Wamsutta Mills; additions were subsequently made, and the plant now contains 100,000 spindles and 2,600 looms, and employs 800 persons on fine cotton goods. In 1883, just south beyond the Potomska Mills the Acushnet Mill was erected, and in the spring of 1888 another one was added, making the combined capacity about 105,000 spindles and 3,400 looms, giving employment to 1,100 persons, and the production consists of a large variety of fine cottons. The New Bedford Manufacturing Company erected a mill in the central portion of the city in 1883, near the water front, for the manufacture of cotton yarns; another mill was erected in 1886, and both factories now contain 37,000 spindles and employ 450 hands. In 1882, the Oneko woolen mill was erected at the North End, half a mile

THE MAMMOTH FACTORY OF THE GRINNELL MANUFACTURING CO.

tion of another cotton manufacturing corporation, the Potomska Mills, in 1871. A four story brick mill, 427 x92 feet, with a large weaving shed 108 x 97 feet, attached, was immediately erected at the extreme south end of the city. In 1877 a second mill was built, four stories in height, 348 x 92 feet. The total capacity of both mills is now 108,000 spindles and 2,700 looms, engaged in the manufacture of lawns, sateens, cretonnes, and print goods, and employing 1,300 operatives. The capital of the corporation is now $1,200,000.

The years 1881-3 witnessed what may with justice be called a boom in the cotton manufacture in New Bedford, the erection of new mills almost doubling the capacity, and putting the city in the front rank in this industry. Four mills were erected, three of them being very large. One of these mills was the Wamsutta No. 6, built in 1882. The Grinnell Mill, a mammoth structure, 666 feet long by 98 feet wide and three stories in height, was built in 1882, near the

beyond the Wamsutta Mills; its capacity is twelve sets of cards, sixty-three looms and 4,500 spindles, but it is at present idle.

Another noticeable increase occurred in 1888-9. The Howland Mills Corporation was organized in 1888, and erected a mill for the manufacture of yarn in the southwest part of the city overlooking Clark's Cove, on land that was practically a waste. A second mill was subsequently added, and the two now contain 80,000 spindles and employs 1,100 hands. This corporation erected a village of houses for its operatives adjoining the mills, and these tenements have all modern conveniences and are model dwellings. The City Manufacturing Company erected a yarn mill on the water front, at the foot of Grinnell Street, in 1888, and began manufacturing in December of that year; the corporation erected another mill in 1892, and the present capacity of the plant is 65,000 spindles, giving employment to 650 person. December, 1888, the

Hathaway Manufacturing Company was organized for the manufacture of fine cotton cloth, and began the erection of a mill of 30,000 spindles just south of the Acushnet Mills; additions and new mills have the North End; the first mill was built the same year and the other soon after and they are engaged in the manufacture of high grade cotton yarns, contain 85,000 spindles and employ 750 operatives.

1,400 looms and employs 350 persons. The Columbia Spinning Co. also erected a mill on Coggeshall street, for the production of high grade hosiery yarns, subsequently added another mill, and now operates 50,000 spindles with 550 employees. The Pierce Manufacturing Co. erected a mill on Belleville avenue north of the Bristol Mill, for the production of fine cotton goods, and the plant now consists of 60,000 spindles, 1,400 looms and gives employment to 575 persons. The Rotch Spinning Co. erected two mills just north of the factories of the Howland Mills Co., for the production of hosiery yarns, and the plant now consist of 50,000 spindles and employs 550 persons. In addition to the factories erected by these four corporations in 1892, the City Manufacturing Co. also erected a mill. In 1895 the Whitman Mill was erected on Riverside avenue, corner of Coffin avenue, at the extreme North End of the city. It is one of the largest factories in the city, has 60,800 spindles, 1,700 looms, employs 850 operatives and its product is cotton novelties. The mill of the Dartmouth Manufacturing Co. was built on Cove street, adjoining the Hathaway Mill at the extreme South End in 1896, contains 60,000 spindles, 1,400 looms, employs 650 operatives, and produces fine cotton goods.

New Bedford at the present time is only excelled by Fall River in the number of her cotton mills and the extent of her cotton manufacture. She has distanced the older cotton manufacturing cities,—Lowell, Lawrence and Manchester,—which were leaders in this manufacture while she was still devoting her best energies to the whale fishery. To-day New Bedford in her 35 mills, owned by fifteen large corporations, operates a million and a quarter spindles and about twenty-two thousand looms, giving employment to 13,000 persons and representing an invested capital of over $13,000,000. The production of the New Bedford mills is of a high class, and a much greater variety of styles and fabrics in fancy and fine cottons is turned out than in Fall River, so that the city on the Acushnet is the leader in fine cotton cloths, pattern goods, specialties and novelties. Without doubt the rapid development of the cotton manufacture in New Bedford has been partly due to the favorable natural conditions here existing, as it is said by experts that the humidity of the atmosphere owing to the nearness of the sea, the influx of the Gulf Stream, and the protection from unfavorable winds, makes the spinning of fine yarns possible.

The factories are chiefly located in two groups, one at the North End and the other at the extreme South End of the city, and the immediate neighborhood in each case forms a thickly populated community, with stores, churches, and a life of its own, that gives each vicinity a semi-independent character, while the central part of the city with its great stores, its halls, theatres and fine modern buildings forms the heart of the whole place. The central portion is the original city, as here the life of the community was wholly centered until the recent great growth of the cotton industry. When the first and second Wamsutta mills were the only cotton factories—before the war of the rebellion- the houses of the operatives formed practically a village by themselves at some distance from the city. Now the North End is, next to the central part, the most important section, and with its own retail and business district forms a very busy community. The South End is not so extensive and busy as the North End, but it also has an important centralized life of its own.

Between the centre of the city and the South End, along South Water street, is a region that in the busy whaling days was inhabited largely by Portuguese sailors and their families, from the Azores Islands. This neighborhood is still the home of these people and their descendants, and retains a somewhat foreign

NEW BEDFORD SAFE DEPOSIT AND TRUST CO. BUILDING
Cor. Acushnet Avenue and William Street.

CITIZENS' NATIONAL BANK BUILDING,
Corner William and North Second Streets

appearance. The city has a large population of colored people, the descendants of many negroes who found refuge here in ante-bellum days through the operations of the Underground Railroad. They live chiefly in the western part on the city on Kempton street and vicinity.

With a great variety of industry brought together by the energy and skill of its inhabitants; with a cosmopolitan population gathered from the isles of the sea, from the centres of European civilization, from the farms of Canada, and from all quarters of the globe, with many diverse influences of race,

language, and custom, but all dominated and controlled by the democratic spirit of American institutions; with such conditions and environments, New Bedford has before her a potential future of great promise and hope.

VII.

Banks and Banking.

The increase of the whaling business after the revolution made the establishing of a bank necessary in New Bedford, and to meet the demand the Bedford Bank was incorporated in 1803 with a capital of $60,000, which was increased in 1804 to $150,000. In 1812 the bank was suspended. For the next four years there was no bank in the town, but in 1816, the Bedford Commercial Bank was established with a capital of $100,000, which was increased in 1821 to $150,000, in 1825 to $250,000, in 1831 to $400,000, and in 1851 to $600,000. December 19, 1864, the Bedford Commercial Bank was organized as the National Bank of Commerce, and in 1874 the capital stock was increased to $1,000,000. The

CUMMINGS BUILDING, SOUTHWEST CORNER OF WILLIAM AND PURCHASE STS.
(Mechanics National Bank.)

FIRST NATIONAL BANK.

bank building on North Water street was erected in 1883, and in 1894 the bank moved into its present commodious quarters, in the Masonic Building, Pleasant street.

The next bank established was the Merchants, organized July 13, 1825, with a capital of $150,000, increased in 1828 to $250,000, in 1831 to $400,000, and in 1851 to $600,000. It was reorganized as the Merchants National Bank Feb. 14, 1865, and in 1866 the capital stock was increased to $1,000,000. In 1893 4 the bank erected the present fine building it now occupies, corner of Purchase and William streets, on the site of Liberty Hall.

The third bank organized was the Mechanics, incorporated Oct. 3, 1831. It was reorganized as a state bank June 3, 1864. The original capital was $200,000, increased in 1854 to $600,000, at which amount it has since remained. In 1894 the bank removed to its new quarters, in the Cummings Building, southwest corner of Williams and Purchase streets.

The Marine Bank was organized April 3, 1832, with a capital of $200,000, increased in 1833 to $300,000, in 1851 to $500,000, and in 1855 to

$600,000. It reorganized under the national bank law in 1864, and was the first bank in the city to do so, from which fact the present name of First National Bank was adopted. In 1866 the capital was increased to $1,000,000, at which amount it now stands.

The Citizens National Bank, now located at the corner of William and North Second streets, was incorporated May 17, 1875, with a capital of $250,000, which was subsequently increased to $500,000.

New Bedford Safe Deposit and Trust Co.

The New Bedford Safe Deposit and Trust Company was incorporated by the legislature of 1887, with a capital stock of $100,000, and authority to increase to $500,000. Business was commenced in June, 1888. In November of the same year the stockholders voted to increase the capital stock to $200,000. At that date the number

NEW BEDFORD INSTITUTION FOR SAVINGS.
NEW BUILDING.

of depositors was one hundred and eighty-two and the deposits amounted to $155,000. At present the company has a surplus of $27,000. The banking rooms are on the northeast corner of William street and Acushnet avenue and the quarters are sumptuous and elegant in every respect. It provides means for the safe deposit of any valuable article, it may be appointed trustee under any will or instrument creating a trust for the care and management of property, under the same circumstances, in the same manner, and subject to the same control by the court having jurisdiction of the same, as in the case of a legally qualified person.

The company acts as an agent for any corporation, city, or town in issuing certificates of stock, bonds, or other evidences of indebtedness, and for the payment of dividends and interest thereon. It also acts as an agent in collecting and disbursing the income on any property which may be placed in its charge.

In addition to the various departments of activity which have been enumerated, the company also does a general banking business, precisely like that of a national bank, except that it issues no bank notes. Deposits of money are received payable by check on presentation, and interest is allowed on daily balances and credited monthly. Special rates of interest are allowed on time deposits. Notes are discounted and collections made the same as at any bank.

The distinctive feature of this institution is its fine vault, which was built by the Hall Safe and Lock Company of Cincinnati, Ohio. It contains four hundred and eighty-nine small safes of various sizes, ranging from two and one-half by four and three-quarter inches to twenty by twenty-four inches. They are uniformly twenty-three inches deep. There are also storage rooms for pictures, silver ware, and jewelry. The officers of the institution are: president, John W. Macomber; cashier, Edmund W. Bourne; directors, John W. Macomber, Rufus A. Soule, Benj. F. Brownell, Lot B. Bates, Stephen A. Brownell, Standish Bourne, Frederic Taber, Lemuel LeBaron Holmes, George C. Hatch, Charles S. Paisler, John A. Macomber, 2d, Joseph Poisson, Charles F. Cushing.

NEW BEDFORD INSTITUTION FOR SAVINGS.
View of Vault and General Department.

NEW BEDFORD INSTITUTION FOR SAVINGS.— BUSINESS DEPARTMENT.

New Bedford Institution for Savings.

The New Bedford Institution for Savings is one of the oldest savings banks in the country and is only antedated in Massachusetts by two similar corporations, the Provident Institution for Savings, which came into existence at Boston in 1816, and the Salem Savings bank, to which articles of incorporation were granted in 1818. It was incorporated in 1825 and the charter contained the names of the following leading citizens: William Rotch, Jr., Gilbert Russell, Cornelius Grinnell, Andrew Robeson, Hayden Coggeshall, Benjamin Rodman, John Avery Parker, Eli Haskell, Richard Williams, George Howland, Joseph Bourne, Abraham Shearman, Jr., William W. Swain, Thomas Rotch, Thomas A. Greene, Charles W. Morgan, Samuel Rodman, Jr., John B. Smith, William C. Nye, Thomas S. Swain, William H. Allen, Lemuel Williams, Jr., John Howland, Jr., Charles H. Warren, William P. Grinnell, Joseph Ricketson, Charles Grinnell, Nathan Bates, John Coggeshall, Jr., James Howland, 2d, and Gideon Howland.

The aim of the institution as stated by the charter was "To provide a mode of enabling industrious mechanics, laborers, seamen, widows, minors and others in moderate circumstances to invest such part of their earnings or property as they can conveniently spare, in a manner which will afford them profit and security."

The institution commenced business on the second floor of the wooden building which still stands on Union street, near the northeast corner of Water street, the room being open and the treasurer in attendance on one day in the week. The first deposit was $50 in amount, and was made on Aug. 15, 1825, by Rhoda E. Wood of Fairhaven. During the first two weeks ten others followed her excellent example, and gave into the care of the new institution $050 in the aggregate. By Dec. 28, deposits amounting to $13,051 had been made by 145 persons. The population at that time was only about 5,000.

The institution erected a building of its own on

NEW BEDFORD INSTITUTION FOR SAVINGS.
Trustees' Room.

Water street in 1883, and occupied it from that time until the edifice on the corner of William and Second streets was finished in 1854. From that time until the present year, the last named structure was the home of the old institution.

The deposits of the institution increased from $1,004,277.05 in 1850 to $13,412,220.57 on July 17, 1897, at a steady and uniform rate. This enormous increase finally rendered the building on the corner of William and Second streets

ornate architectural features. The facade on Union street is the most beautiful portion of the design and consists of a colonnade of six pure Corinthian columns, supported by an arcade of of three arches with massive piers and crowned by a pediment which contains a sculptured group of three figures. The central figure represents the protecting spirit of the institution. In her hands she bears the palm and cornucopia, emblems of success and prosperity, and her outspread wings on one hand overshadow the work-

MERCHANTS BANK BUILDING, COR. OF WILLIAM AND PURCHASE STREETS.

inadequate for the needs of the institution. Accordingly at a special meeting of the trustees May 31, 1895, it was voted to authorize the board of investment to purchase a lot at the southeast corner of Fourth and Union streets, as a site for a new building. Action was at once taken, and a contract was made late in 1895 with F. Noyes Whitcomb & Co. of Boston to erect a building from the design submitted by Chas. Brigham of Boston. The building was in process of construction during 1896, and was completed and occupied by the institution June 28, 1897.

The new structure is a striking and attractive building, massive and solid until in form. The design is somewhat severe, but it is relieved by a number of

man at his anvil and on the other the widow and her child. This work of art is by Mr. Hugh Cairnes of Boston.

The building is entirely isolated from all the surrounding structures, thus ensuring safety from fire and burglars. In shape it is rectangular, the frontage on Union street being 53 feet 8 inches, and the depth on Fourth street street 91 feet 9 inches; and the extreme height from the sidewalk is 58 feet. It is constructed of stone from the Bedford quarries of Indiana. In its interior arrangements the building is admirably adapted to the requirements of the institution. The banking room occupies the greater portion of the interior, its dimensions being 48 feet in width by 53 feet 6 inches in length, and 47 feet 6 inches in height, extending nearly to the roof. The walls are lined with Sienna marble to a height of about 16 feet in regular ashlar work, of absolute simplicity, devoid of all moulding or paneling, and above the ashlar are treated with a series of Corinthian pilasters, symmetrically arranged and supporting a heavily paneled ceiling, whose deep compartments are richly though not profusely ornamented. Between these pilasters are the nine great circular-headed windows of the exterior, three on each of the principal sides, the

and enclosure are the great safes or vaults of the institution, and on the right hand, towards Fourth street, is conveniently located the treasurer's room. Adjoining it is a room for the president and board of investment, 14 feet 6 inches by 22 feet 8 inches, lighted from Fourth street, having a convenient dressing room and lavatory.

The present officers are: president, William W. Crapo; vice-presidents, Edward D. Mandell and Horatio Hathaway; treasurer, Charles H. Pierce; assistant-treasurer, F. A. Washburn; secretary, William G. Wood.

The building is one of the best appointed banking

INTERIOR SANDERS & BARROWS' CLOTHING CO., MERCHANTS BANK BUILDING.

fourth being treated in harmony. In the centre of the ceiling a rectangular dome terminates in a ceiling light of unusual dimensions, which, together with the nine large windows of the exterior walls amply lights every portion of the interior. A gallery with a wrought iron balustrade of light and delicate tracery extends all round the room and gives access to the various windows and to the balcony on the front.

In the centre of the room is the counting house. At the various delivery openings are bronze screens or gates. The counter which surrounds the enclosure and the various tables and desks which constitute its furniture are of mahogany. At the rear of the room

offices in the country. It is an object of interest to all, and affords a lesson in taste by its beauty and in thrift by its character.

The New Bedford Five Cents Saving was incorporated May 5, 1855, and the present fine building at 37 Purchase street was erected in 1892.

Sanders & Barrows Clothing Co.

The business house of the Sanders & Barrows Clothing Co., which has now grown to be a modern emporium, was started in 1806 by William Sanders at 108 Union street. Here it remained until 1878 when it was transferred into the Waite Block, William street.

At that time a brother of the founder, Henry V. Sanders, was admitted to partnership, and this arrangement continued until 1881, when he retired and Frank C. Barrows, who had long been a clerk in the store, became a member of the firm, which then assumed the style of Sanders & Barrows.

The business continued to be carried on in the Waite Block until 1894, when it was removed into the handsome building of the Merchants Bank then just erected on the site of Liberty Hall. At that time the concern was incorporated under the name of the

The present officers of the company are: William Sanders, treasurer and general manager; Frank C. Barrows, president; John H. Barrows, clerk of the corporation; directors— William Sanders, Frank C. Barrows, John H. Barrows, E. H. Farr, all of New Bedford; and Charles H. Chase, of Boston.

Both Mr. Sanders and Mr. Barrows have been unusually prominent in public affairs. The former represented New Bedford in the Legislature in 1879 and 1880; was superintendent of city cemeteries for six years; chairman of cemetery board for two years;

BRISTOL COUNTY COURT HOUSE, COUNTY STREET.

Sanders & Barrows Clothing Co., with a capital stock of $50,000. The new quarters were elegantly fitted up and at present compare favorably with those of any similar establishment in any leading city. The main store is 80 by 80 feet and is lighted on the front by three mammoth plate glass windows, and at the rear by a large skylight. The total floor area of the establishment including the basement, which is used for storage, is about 14,000 feet. A large stock of the best quality and style of men's, youths' and children's clothing, hats, caps, gentlemen's furnishings, underclothing, neckwear, etc., is constantly carried, and the reputation of the company for courtesy and fair dealing is unsurpassed.

has been county commissioner since 1889 and chairman for 1896-7. He was commander of the New Bedford City Guards for ten years; is a veteran of the civil war, and a member of G. A. R. Post No. 1. He is an Odd Fellow, and has been twice regent of Omega Council of the Royal Arcanum. He is an ardent member of the L. A. W. and has been a director of the Board of Trade for ten years. Mr. Barrows served as overseer of the poor for five years, was a member of the common council in 1890, and an alderman in 1893-4. He is a Mason, an Odd Fellow, belongs to the Royal Arcanum, and is a member of the Dartmouth and Union Clubs. He was a lieutenant in the New Bedford City Guards for a number of years.

SANFORD & KELLEY, BANKERS.

present firm. The house transacts a general investment business, and has always had the confidence and patronage of the leading New Bedford capitalists. A private wire connects the house with correspondents in Boston, and by this means telegraphic communication is maintained with New York, Philadelphia, Chicago, Providence, and other centres. The firm was the first in New Bedford to lease a private wire. Both Mr. Sanford and Mr. Kelley are members of the Boston Stock Exchange, and they are also stock auctioneers.

For many years the banking rooms were at 47 North Water street, in conveniently arranged and well appointed quarters. That neighborhood was then the financial centre of the city, and consequently the firm was within its limits, and able to enjoy the advantages of being in the proper

Sanford & Kelley.

The leading private bankers in New Bedford are Sanford & Kelley, whose banking house is located in the new building at 21 Pleasant street. The business was established in 1848 by Edward L. Baker, who was a man of considerable financial ability. He it was who disposed of the majority of the stock of the first Wamsutta cotton mill. Mr. Baker sold out to Samuel P. Burt, his confidential clerk, in 1865. In 1875, Mr. Burt took as partners, Gardner T. Sanford and Charles S. Kelley, under the firm name of S. P. Burt & Co., Mr. Burt being located in Milwaukee, Wis. On the death of Mr. Burt in the West, in 1884, the surviving partners formed the

environment. But with the changes that the past few years have brought about, the relocation of the banks on the upper streets, the decadence of the fishery

SANFORD & KELLEY--BANKING ROOMS.

interest and the increased prominence of manufactur
ing, a new location became necessary. Accordingly, the
members of the firm had the building they now occupy
erected on their own specifications, by this plan securing offices in every way suitable for their business.
The total dimensions of the new quarters, which
are on the ground floor, are 50 x 33 feet, and the
rooms consists of a main office, divided about equally
between a reading and reception room for customers,
and space reserved for the partners and the office
force. In the rear of this main apartment is a large
private office, and also
toilet rooms and lavato-
ries. A large plate glass
window affords ample
light at the front, while
a skylight provides a
natural illumination in
the rear. The offices are
fitted with excellent
taste. The firm moved
into these quarters Sep-
tember 21, 1891.

For some years San-
ford & Kelley compiled
and issued annually a
little pocket compen-
dium of about eighty
pages, containing inter-
esting statistics about
the cotton and other
manufactures, the city's
finances, banks, popula-
tion, etc.; also a sum-
mary of the city's history,
paragraphs recounting
the city's advantages,
and many other mat-
ters of interest. This
was a very useful and
handy book, and was a
material help in advanc-
ing the interest of the city. The last issue of this
book was in 1893, but an abridged form, in a booklet
of sixteen pages, was issued in 1896.

George B. Richmond.

For many years, late in the 60's and early in the 70's
the most conspicuous man in New Bedford was
George B. Richmond. He was a radical temperance
man, believed in the suppression of the liquor traffic
by political means, and showed his faith by his works
in an effective way by organizing and leading those
who agreed with him repeatedly to victory. He was
the general in the great contests which raged during
that period, and although repeatedly defeated he was
five times elected mayor of the city on the temperance
issue, and held the office in 1870, 1871, 1872, 1874
and 1878. His administration was aggressive, and

the laws against liquor selling were probably better
enforced under his direction than they had been up
to that period or indeed have since been in any city
in the commonwealth. In other respects his conduct
of city affairs was highly satisfactory and painstaking
and many improvements were carried out in street
extensions, the building of schoolhouses, and in other
respects.

Mr. Richmond was born in New Bedford Nov. 9,
1821. He was educated at the Friends Academy,
New Bedford, Pierce Academy, Middleboro, and spent
two years at Brown Uni-
versity, Providence, but
was obliged to discon-
tinue his studies on
account of ill health. He
then returned to New
Bedford and engaged in
business life. In 1851
he was elected on the
Whig ticket as a mem-
ber of the state legisla-
ture of 1852. May 1,
1861, he was appointed
inspector, w e i g h e r,
gauger and measurer in
the New Bedford Cus-
tom house and held the
office until he resigned
in 1874. For some years
during the seventies he
was a member of the
state police commission.
In 1880 he represented
the third Bristol County
district in the Massa-
chusett senate. In
1883 he was appointed
Registrar of Deeds for
the Southern Bristol
District, and this posi-
tion he still holds, his

HON. GEORGE B. RICHMOND.

office being in the Court House on County street.
He has held many other official positions on com-
missions, was long an active member of the state
county, district and city Republican committees, has
been connected with most of the leading charitable
and beneficial institutions of the city, and has been
in all ways a conscientious, honest and public
spirited citizen.

Mr. Richmond has the honor at this celebration of
the fiftieth year of the city's existence, of being the
oldest living ex-mayor. His hearty approval and
support of the work of the Semi-Centennial committee in bringing this matter to a successful
issue, has very materially aided in the undertaking
to make this celebration and the industrial exhibition
that accompanies it, as perfect as any that have been
held in New England.

George L. Brownell.

The longest established and the largest carriage manufacturing business in New Bedford is conducted by George L. Brownell, in an extensive plant, corner of Cannon street and Acushnet avenue. A specialty is made of the manufacture of fine hearses, coaches and undertaker's wagons, but light carriages of every description are also made.

Mr. Brownell, who was born in Westport, began to learn the trade of a carriage maker in New Bedford when he was 17 years old, in the shop of Ayres R. Marsh. After completing his apprenticeship in 1843, he bought his employer's business. In 1846 increasing business led him to make extensive additions to his shop. In 1853 he built a new shop on Third street. About this time he commenced the manufacture of

yard, the entire buildings covering an area of 17,160 feet, and finally a warehouse was built on Acushnet avenue, 75 by 40 feet in area, and three stories high. The factory is now one of the largest in the country, and gives employment to between 50 and 100 men.

The manufacturing plant covers an entire square, and comprises the factory, blacksmith's shop, wood-working department, painting and trimming department, and six large repositories, where a full assortment of hearses, undertakers' wagons, ambulances, and embalming buggies are constantly on hand. Mr. Brownell also deals in both heavy and light carriages, and has a large variety of second-hand hearses from which to make selections. The trade has been extensive throughout the New England and Middle States, and large shipments have also been made to

CARRIAGE FACTORY OF GEORGE L. BROWNELL,
Corner Cannon Street and Acushnet Avenue.

hearses. In 1863 the business had increased to such an extent that further accommodations were required, and he bought the stone building at the corner of Third and Cannon streets, formerly occupied by Samuel Leonard & Son in the manufacture of oil. This building was refitted, and was ready for occupancy Nov. 12, 1863, on which date Mr. Brownell entertained 1,500 of his friends and fellow-townsmen at a public dedication of the establishment.

The original stone building is a two-and-a-half story structure of stone, 100 feet long by 60 wide. But the constant increase in the business soon rendered additional buildings necessary. First an addition, two stories high and thirty feet wide was built, extending from the main structure, a distance of 130 feet, on Cannon street. Then a second wing was built, and two large buildings were erected in the

5-H

foreign countries. Since the business was established, over $5,000,000 worth of carriages have been sold.

Notwithstanding his advanced age, Mr. Brownell is still to be found at the works every day, giving his personal attention to the various details of the immense business.

S. S. Paine & Brother.

One of the oldest, if not indeed the very oldest merchant now engaged in business in New Bedford is Samuel S. Paine, the senior partner of the firm of S. S. Paine & Brother, dealers in brick, lime, cement and builders' materials. He is a native of Bristol, R. I., came to New Bedford in 1830 when a boy of 16, and went to work in a grocery store conducted by a man from his native place. Returning home in 1833, he remained in Bristol a few months, working

MASONIC BUILDING AND VIEW OF PLEASANT STREET.

Acushnet River, Union street has been the centre of the business of the place. At first a cartpath leading from the few houses on the hill to the shore, it became a village street lined with stores and shops. The houses of the leading merchants were on the upper parts of the street and their business places on the lower portions. The "Four Corners" at the intersection of Union and Water streets, was in the early years of the century the centre of the town. The street still maintains much of its old importance, and

in his father's store, but in response to the invitation of Captain John P. West, to whom his first employer had recommended him, he returned to New Bedford and became Captain West's clerk. This position he held for five years when Captain West took him into partnership, and the firm became known as West & Paine. In addition to the building material business they were also whaling merchants, and were agents for two vessels. About 1845 the partnership was dissolved, Captain West taking the whaling business as his share and Mr. Paine the building material business. In 1860 Mr. Paine's younger brother, George W. Paine, became a partner, and the style of the firm thereafter was S. S. Paine & Brother.

The business of the firm is now carried on at the old location on Front street and connected with the premises is a commodious dock and wharf.

Mr. Paine is a man of marked strength of character, strictly honorable, consistent and upright in all his dealings, and has always manifested the best traits of the New England Puritan, without the harshness and sternness that are sometimes unjustly ascribed to that type.

Union Street.

Since the time when Joseph Russell established himself on the shores of the

the illustration below shows its present appearance at the junction with Purchase and Fourth streets, which is now the centre of the city.

The Masonic Building at the corner of Union and Pleasant streets, and the bank building of the New Bedford Institution for Savings, at the corner of Union and Purchase streets, are among the finest structures in the city. These, together with the Opera House and a few other new buildings, have very much improved the appearance of Union street, as well as enhancing the value of property.

UNION STREET, LOOKING WEST.

F. W. Wentworth Co.

One of the finest and best appointed of the first class retail establishments in New Bedford is that of the F. W. Wentworth Co., occupying the first floor and basement of the Masonic building, corner of Union and Pleasant streets. The company carries a fine line of ready-made clothing of the very best grades, and is sole agent in New Bedford for Rogers, Peet & Co., whose reputation as makers of high-class and well fitting garments is not surpassed by any other

agent for the celebrated and popular Dunlap hats. In the basement a trunk department is conducted, which is well stocked with a full line of ladies' and gentlemen's trunks, hand bags, valises, dress suit cases, etc.

The F. W. Wentworth Co. was established three years ago. With a new business, new goods, and new fixtures, it was the first tenant to occupy the quarters in the new Masonic building that are still the head quarters of the company.

From the first the business has been a success.

INTERIOR OF THE F. W. WENTWORTH CO.'S STORE.

New Bedford Gas and Edison Light Co.

The New Bedford Gas Co. was incorporated in 1850, with a capital of $50,000 under a charter granted by the state of Massachusetts. The principal projectors were a number of Philadelphia capitalists, but two well known New Bedford men were associated with them— Abraham Howland, first mayor of the city, and James B. Congdon, city clerk. In a short time the interests of the Philadelphia gentlemen were bought out by local capitalists, and a permanent organization

their respective positions, Mr. Congdon until his death, and Mr. Taber resigned a year or two after his associate passed away. Gilbert Allen was elected to fill both positions and remained in office until 1890.

The Gas Company having been granted permission by the State Gas Commission in March, 1888, to manufacture and sell electricity for light and power, it purchased the property of the New Bedford Electric Light Company, which was then furnishing arc lights to the city from a station at the foot of School street. To provide for this purchase and make subsequent improvements the capital stock was increased to $300,000. Four Westinghouse incandescent dynamos

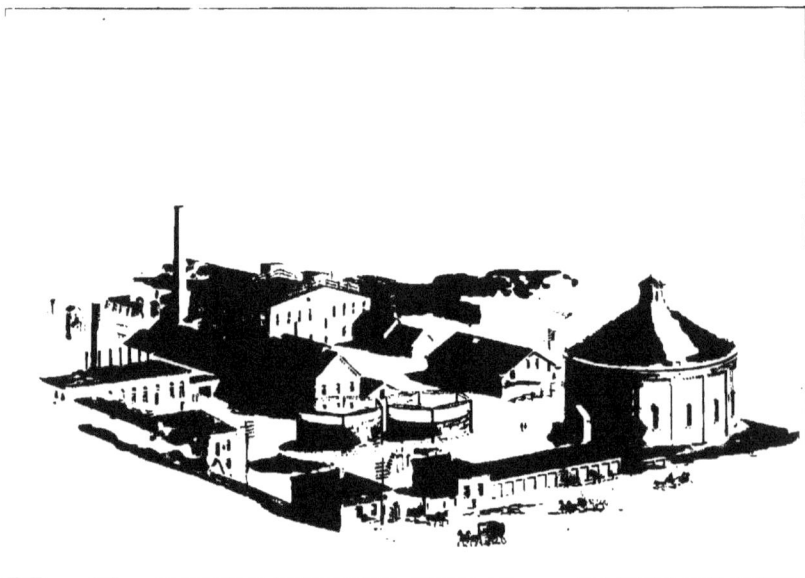

BIRD'S-EYE VIEW OF THE PLANT OF THE NEW BEDFORD GAS & EDISON LIGHT CO.

was effected, with William C. Taber as president, and James B. Congdon as treasurer.

The construction of a plant was at once begun, and on Feb. 14, 1853, the works were completed and the gas turned on. As first erected the entire plant occupied but a small part of the present location, between Water street and the harbor, at the foot of Madison, then called Bush street, and consisted of a brick retort house, a small gas holder of the capacity of 35,000 cubic feet, an office and a coal shed. Additions and enlargements have been made until over four acres are occupied, and the storage capacity of the three holders is about 200,000 cubic feet, the annual sale being over 70,000,000 cubic feet. To meet these expenditures the capital stock was gradually increased up to the year 1888 to $225,000.

For over 30 years Messrs. Congdon and Taber held

of a capacity of 2,000 lamps of 16-candle power were added to the plant a few years after the Gas Company acquired it.

At this time, however the Gas Company had a rival in the electric lighting field. The Edison Electric Light Co., organized in 1884 on the basis of a capital of $100,000, began the construction of a two story brick building on Middle street, Oct. 9, 1885, and the plant was started Jan. 28, 1886. The plant consisted of a 150 and an 80 horse power engine, two 100 horse power boilers, two number 20 Edison incandescent dynamos and two number 8 dynamos, with a capacity of 2,400 16-candle power lights. About 600 lights were wired for when the current was turned on.

Afterwards the plant was increased by four number 20 dynamos and two number 32 dynamos, increasing the lighting capacity to 10,500 lamps.

The consolidation of the New Bedford Electric Light Co. with the Gas Company had been strongly opposed at the public hearings by the Edison Electric Light

CHAS. S. PAISLER'S OFFICE AND STORAGE PLANT,
No. North Water Street

16-candle power lamps. About 300 horse power of motors are also supplied by the company. In 1891 the company installed a water gas plant at their works. This plant has a capacity of about 300,000 feet per day.

New Bedford's streets are now lighted by about 525 gas lamps, 200 arc lamps and several circuits of incandescent lamps furnished by this company, which also supplies Fairhaven with 85 electric lights for the streets; the public buildings and many residences are also lighted from this company's works.

The offices of the company are at the former head-quarters of the Edison Electric Co. on Middle street. The present officers of the company are: president, George R. Stetson; treasurer and clerk, Charles R. Price; directors, Gilbert Allen, Horatio Hathaway, Horace G. Howland, David B. Kempton, George F. Kingman, Thomas H. Knowles, John P. Knowles, Jr., Charles H. Lawton, John W. Macomber, Andrew G. Pierce, Charles R. Price, George R. Stetson, Frederick Taber. The capital stock of the company is $550,000.

tion. Mr. Paisler erected in 1879 the present commodious two-story brick building he occupies. It is very favorably situated, being directly on the harbor in the rear, and the materials are received both by rail and vessel. Mr. Paisler has been awarded some of the largest contracts in the city for building material, among which the following are some of the most important, viz.: the High School building, all the Grammar School buildings, the Fire Department engine houses, fifteen of the large cotton mills erected during the past ten years, the Odd Fellows building, Grace Church, St. Lawrence Church, the Five Cent Savings Bank building, the Citizens Bank building, Cushing building, the building for the Union for Good Works, and many others. Mr. Paisler is a popular citizen, takes a great interest in public affairs, and is a very genial and pleasant gentleman.

GEO. DELANO'S SONS' OIL WORKS, SOUTH AND SO. SECOND STREETS.

George Delano's Sons.

The oil refinery of George Delano's Sons, at the corner of South and South Second streets, is one of the most important industrial plants in New Bedford. The buildings cover nearly two acres of land, and in the busy season forty-five men are employed. The business is one of the oldest in the city, and the refinery is among the largest of its kind in the country. It was first started by George T. Baker, subsequently passed into the hands of Oliver and George O. Crocker, and about 1856 became the property of Charles H. Leonard. George Delano entered the employ of Mr. Leonard in 1855, and on January 1, 1860, became the owner of the business. He was succeeded in 1884 by his sons, Stephen C. and James Delano, who have since conducted the plant under the present name. The concern has an office and salesroom at 176 Front street, New York. The firm manufactures sperm, whale, sea elephant, fish, and cotton seed oils, patent and paraffine wax candles, sperm oil, whale and fish oil pressings, and sperm and whale oil soap. All crude oils are worked out to definite results at the factory, and the product is shipped to every part of the world.

Isaac C. Sherman & Son.

The oldest wholesale house engaged in the sale of fruit and produce in New Bedford is that of Messrs. Isaac C. Sher-

man & Son, whose senior partner established the business as long ago as the year 1847. He admitted his son, Mr. Edward D. Sherman to partnership in 1876, when the firm assumed its present name. The large four-story building at 70 to 76 Union street, is with the exception of the upper story, all utilized in the business, the first floor for a salesroom and office, the second floor entirely for bananas, of which this firm makes a specialty, handling the Boston Fruit Co's account for this city; and the third story and basement for storage purpose. An elevator connects the various floors. A very large stock of foreign and domestic fruits and produce is constantly kept on hand. This house is always prepared to supply the trade at the lowest market rates,

I. C. SHERMAN & SON'S WHOLESALE FRUIT HOUSE,
Page 50

W. A. ROBINSON & CO.'S OIL WORKS, SOUTH WATER AND FRONT STREETS.

W. A. Robinson & Co.

W. A. Robinson & Co. are among the largest refiners of Sperm and Whale Oil in this country. This firm was established in Rhode Island in 1820, but transferred its business to New Bedford in 1853. In 1863 the firm moved to the stone factory it now occupies, No. 144 South Water street, which it has occupied for 34 years. The main building is two stories high, with a frontage of 40 feet on Water street. It is connected with smaller buildings of brick and stone, extending to Front street, a distance of 240 feet. There are large sheds for storing oil on Walnut street, south of the factory buildings. The buildings are lighted by gas and heated by steam, and employment is given to fifteen or twenty hands. The manufacture and sale of Sperm and Whale Oils and their products is the principal business, although the firm deals largely in other oils.

The sons of New Bedford made the whale fishing a great business gave to it a national importance and when that occupation failed through natural causes and changes in industrial conditions, they branched out as manufacturers, and, in the course of two decades, such was their energy that as a manufacturing centre the city has quickly come to the front rank.

and numbers among its regular customers the leading retail dealers in the city, while its country trade also forms a material factor of the general business. By strict attention to business aided by their experience, enterprise, and integrity, both partners fully justify the unanimous opinion of their reliability and trustworthiness which is held concerning them. Mr. Isaac C. Sherman was born in Rochester, Mass., while his son and copartner first saw the light in New Bedford.

Frank M. Douglass.

Frank M. Douglass, the proprietor of the centrally located drug store, on the south-east corner of Fifth and Union streets, was born in New Bedford in 1854. He received his education in the public schools, and at the age of 14 began to learn the business of an apothecary with Elisha Thornton, Jr. After completing his apprenticeship he went to Boston, and worked in the drug store of H. A. Choate, under the Revere House. Returning to New Bedford, he was employed by Wm. P. S. Cadwell and his successor, Frank R. Hadley, up to 1882, at which time he purchased from H. W. Parker his present store. This was an old stand as a drug store, and Mr. Douglass has made a great success of the business. He carries a first-class line of drugs, medicines, toilet and fancy articles; carefully compounds prescriptions, and is favored with a first-class trade.

DRUG STORE OF F. M. DOUGLASS, COR. FIFTH AND UNION STREETS.

MORSE TWIST DRILL AND MACHINE CO.

MANSION HOUSE, UNION STREET.

The Mansion House.

The well known hotel, the Mansion House, corner of Union and Second streets was originally the residence of William Rotch, and was erected early in the century. It was opened as a hotel, Dec. 18, 1828, by J. Webster. Louis Boutelle conducted it for many years. A large addition was made to the north end in 1887, and in 1891, extensive alterations were made in the interior of the hotel, connecting it with the building just east which now forms part of it.

Mr. C. W. Ripley became proprietor in 1885, and conducted the house for a number of years. He was succeeded by F. B. Carr, who in turn was succeeded by the present proprietors, Benjamin Dawson and Stephen A. Brownell, who took possession of the house in 1895. Under the control of these enterprising business men, with Mr. F. E. McMackin as manager, the hotel has been very prosperous and is now well patronized.

The Mansion House is centrally and conveniently located, and, although the main part is an old building, still presents a fine appearance. An annex was built on the Second street end, six years ago, and this addition contains twenty rooms, modern in size and appointments. The entire house has over sixty rooms, all comfortably furnished, lighted and well ventilated. The dining room has a seating capacity

6-w

for fifty persons, while the parlors, public rooms, and other apartments for visitors are commodious and convenient. Annunciators are placed in every bedroom, the telephone is free to patrons, and every comfort and convenience known to modern hotel-keeping are provided for guests. The house is heated by steam throughout with a radiator in every room. The cuisine is excellent, and every effort is made to make patrons comfortable. There is a barber shop in the basement, bathrooms, closets, etc., are upon every floor, and fire-escapes permit a ready means of exit. Prices will always be found reasonable, the ruling rates being two dollars per day.

Taber, Read & Gardner.

One of the firms that dates back to the busy whaling days, and which is still a prosperous and energetic concern under the new conditions, is Taber, Read & Gardner, dealers in clothing and gentlemen's furnishings, at the corner of Union street and

TABER, READ & GARDNER, CLOTHING AND GENTS' FURNISHING STORE, Cor. Union Street and Acushnet Avenue.

Acushnet avenue. The house was established in 1850 by Joseph R. Read and Edward T. Taber, under the name of Taber, Read & Co. In 1868 Darius P. Gardner was admitted as a partner, and the firm then assumed its present title of Taber, Read & Gardner. Mr. Read died in 1879, and his son, William F. Read, then succeeded to his interest, and since then has been the active manager of the business. Mr. Taber died in 1883. Of the old members of the firm, Mr. Gardner is the only one remaining. In the old days the firm were agents for whaling vessels, and did a large business as outfitters. The main business of the house has always been clothing and gentlemen's furnishings, hats, caps, underclothing and neckwear, and it is still a leader in these lines, carrying an extensive and varied stock of first-class goods. Mr. W. F. Read has had many years experience, both with the old firm, and also in Boston.

Stephen A. Brownell.

A man who has filled a large place in the recent history of New Bedford is Stephen A. Brownell. He has been active both in business and public life, is a leading merchant, was mayor of the city in 1894, and is Vice-Chairman of the Committee that has charge of the Semi-Centennial Celebration. Owing to the illness of Mayor Ashley, he has been Acting Chairman, has presided at nearly all the meetings and has been the executive head of the Celebration. He was born in Westport, Jan. 5, 1844, and was educated in the common schools of his native town and at Pierce Academy, Middleboro. He then taught country schools for four terms, after which he was a storekeeper in and the postmaster of Central Village in Westport from 1864 to 1870. Subsequently for six years he was engaged in the live cattle trade, to which was soon added the slaughtering of cattle. He came to New Bedford in April, 1878, and was first employed here by Pardon Cornell, wholesale meat dealer, as manager. He remained in this position six years, then became a partner in the business, and six years later succeeded to the entire business of P. Cornell & Co., becoming the New Bedford agent of P. D. Armour & Co., of Chicago. His business has been conducted under the style of Stephen A. Brownell. Meanwhile he engaged in numerous other enterprises, including manufacturing and banking. He is now a director of the Dartmouth and Westport Electric Railroad, the New Bedford Safe Deposit and Trust Co., and the New Bedford Co-operative Bank; president and director of the Strange Forged Drill & Tool Co.; president of the New Bedford Board of Trade, and member of the Ancient and Honorable Artillery Co., of Boston, Mass.

His public life was begun while he was a resident of Westport, as a member of the lower house of the Legislature. In New Bedford he was elected a member of the City Council in 1886-87, and Alderman in 1888-90-91-92; Mayor, 1894. He belongs to all the leading Masonic orders in the city, and is a Thirty-Second Degree Mason; is also a member of American Order of United Workmen, New Bedford Order of Benevolent Elks, the Acushnet Lodge of Odd Fellows, Stella Lodge, Daughters of Rebecca; President and Director of Odd Fellows Building Association of New Bedford; a member of the Hunters' Club of New Bedford, Mayors' Club of Massachusetts, and the Club of Legislature of 1870.

Mr. Brownell is properly called the father of New Bedford's extensive Public Park System. He has done more to develop public sentiment in this direction and accomplished more in locating and improving Public Parks than any other citizen. It has been a special hobby of his for the last 15 years and it is gratifying to witness the results of his efforts.

ARMOUR & CO.'S NEW BUILDING.

For many years Mr. Brownell's business has been conducted in a group of old buildings at the foot of School street, but he will move about the second week in October, 1897, into a new building on the east side of Front street, between Union and Central streets, which has just been completed by Armour & Co. The building is a substantial structure of brick, 90 feet long by 57 feet wide, two lofty stories in height, with a seven foot basement. The height of the edifice, from the level of the sidewalk to the eaves, is 36 feet.

This structure is designed as a storehouse and a receiving and distributing depot for meats and the products of Armour & Co., for whom Mr. Brownell's firm are sole agents in New Bedford, and it has been constructed with all the care that the wide and extensive experience of the great Chicago packers renders possible. The building is a solid block, with the exception of a square space, occupying the half of the front on the lower story, which is open, and de-

signed for a covered shipping way for wagons to back up and receive goods. Platforms extend around it along the walls, and it can be entered from Front street or the side street.

The offices and salesrooms are on the first floor front, and are beautifully finished in polished oak. They are lighted by large plate glass windows. The remainder of the first floor is divided into three compartments, the smoked meat room, the pickling room, and the "cooler." The latter is in reality the refrigerator, is the largest room in the building, and

so as to be perfectly water tight, it is thought. The floor is only a few inches above ordinary high tides but not above spring and neap tides, consequently there is danger that the water may at times be forced in. While this is not expected, provision has been made to run the water off in case of such a disaster by outlets in the floor connected with pipes, and protected by strong screw caps. The basement will be used for barrel storage of pickled meats, etc

A hydraulic elevator in the rear of the office connects the basement with the second story. A spur

ARMOUR & CO.'S NEW PLANT, FRONT STREET.

is used as a store house for "fresh cuts" of meat. The beef is suspended from lines of overhead railways, which run out into the salesroom and driveway at the front, and on to the shipping platform in the rear, and by their means the carcasses are received and delivered readily and easily. The temperature in the "cooler" is maintained at 30 degrees F.

In the space in the second story over the "cooler" are the ice bunkers, capable of holding 300 tons of ice. This is the ice box of the "cooler," and the whole thus forms an immense refrigerator. The other portions of the second story are devoted to storage, etc., and in the front are lavatories and toilet rooms. On the front and sides of this portion are large plate glass windows.

The basement of the building presents some unique features. It is seven feet high, is cemented

track runs close up to the rear of the building so that meats can be landed directly on the platform, and run by the overhead railway into the "cooler," while a skid provides for the passage of barrels into the basement.

When Mr. Brownell moves into this building, Mr. John W. Bannister, who has been connected with the business for sixteen years, and is now manager, will become a partner.

Parker House.

For many years the Parker House on Purchase street, in the centre of the city, has been a well known hotel. It was first opened as a hotel on February 10, 1842, by Horton & Son, and has ever since been a public house. It was formerly the residence of John Avery Parker, a prominent merchant, but many additions have been made to the original structure.

William Baylies.

One of the old-time commercial houses whose chief business was the provisioning of ships, but which has survived and adapted its energies to changed conditions is that conducted by William Baylies at 8 to 16 Union street, on the water front. The business was established in 1833, by Alexander H. Seabury & Co., and from the first was carried on in the present building, a substantial three-story structure of stone, which was then erected for its accommodation by Mr. Seabury. William Baylies went to work for Mr. Seabury,

ever, especially in the last two decades, all this was changed.

While the house still is prepared to supply ships, a large general wholesale business in flour and grain was developed as the returns from the whale ships dwindled. Within the past few years an extensive line of groceries has been added, and at present Mr. Baylies is a general wholesale merchant in flour, grain and groceries.

Several specialties are handled. The house is the sole packer of Baylies' Rolled Oats; is the sole agent

WILLIAM BAYLIES' GRAIN AND FLOUR ESTABLISHMENT
No. 800 Union street.

as a clerk, in 1845, and in 1849, when Mr. Seabury retired, he, in company with Nathaniel C. Cannon, became the owners, and conducted the business under the firm name of Baylies & Cannon. Mr. Baylies was the manager. Mr. Cannon died in 1876, and since then the house has been conducted under Mr. Baylies' name alone. Two of Mr. Baylies' sons now have an interest in the business, C. S. Baylies, who became a partner in 1885, and R. L. Baylies, who entered the firm in 1887.

The original business of the house was to supply whale ships with provisions for a voyage, and in the heyday of the whale fishery this required a large capital, the dealings were extensive and the returns were good. With the decline of whaling, how-

for the Roller Mills first quailty of fancy flour manufactured by Christian Bros. & Co., Minneapolis; and is wholesale agent for Bloomer Club 5 cent cigar and Plutocrat 10 cent cigar. The sale of these specialties is all under the control of Logan R. Doane.

Mr. Baylies is heavily interested in whaling vessels, and owns large shares of the following: Steamer William Baylies (named after him, and of which a picture is shown on page 8); steamer Belvedere; barks Horatio, California, Alice Knowles, Canton, Platina, Greyhound; schooners Pedro Varela and Joseph G. Dean. William Lewis and J. & W. R. Wing are agents for most of these vessels, which, with the exception of the Pedro Varela, are now all out on voyages.

BUILDING OF THE W. S. HILL ELECTRIC CO.

W. S. Hill Electric Co.

The W. S. Hill Electric Co., manufacturers of switches, switchboards, panel boards, fuse blocks and electrical supplies, was established in New Bedford in 1896. The business was transferred to this city from Boston, where it was established many years ago by Mr. W. S. Hill, one of the pioneers in the construction of electrical appliances and devices. The plant is now operated in the large three-story brick building, No. 10 Elm street, and occupies three floors 150 x 100 feet. A foundry has recently been added, by which the company is enabled to get out its product much more speedily than formerly. No poor castings are allowed to enter into any part of the construction, but every one is thoroughly tested.

During the past year the company has installed, despite the hard times, some of the largest switchboards now in use in this country. Among these have been one in the Congressional Library, Washington, D. C., and one in the Public Library, Boston, Mass. Recently they installed a large switchboard of beautiful white Italian marble in the Hotel Tourraine, Boston, and a similar one in the American House in the same city. Orders for these switchboards are received from all parts of the country.

Several lines of switches are manufactured, which cannot be excelled by any others on the market. The most important of these is the "Standard Reinforced Contact Switch," which is the "Hill Switch" improved. Another switch greatly in demand is the "All-copper Switch." Besides these, "Single Break" and "Quick Break" Switches in all sizes are manufactured. The company also does a great deal of special switch work, and manufactures special switch appliances to order. Recently there was made at the factory, on a special order, a "Booster Short Circuit Switch" of 2,000 amperes, designed to throw in and out a "Booster" dynamo for increasing voltage at extreme ends of long circuits.

The large switchboard, a picture of which is shown on this page, which was installed at the Utica State Hospital, Utica, N. Y., is made of black polished slate, with the very finest japanned iron grill work at bottom, and fancy, solid, polished brass pedestals, all of the very highest finish. A similar board has been installed in the Syracuse (N. Y.) State Institution for Feeble Minded Children.

The present officers of the W. S. Hill Electric Co. are: F. A. Sowle, President; Caleb Hammond, Vice-President; C. S. Mendell, Treasurer and Manager. The company is incorporated under the laws of Massachusetts and is capitalized for $70,000.

BOSTON BEEF CO.

Operates Three Stores.—Leads in Meats and Groceries.

The largest concern dealing in meats and groceries at retail at the present time in New Bedford is the Boston Beef Co., which runs three stores in different parts of the city. The business was originally started September 28, 1891, at the North End, but the field there was not found large enough, and the

SWITCHBOARD
AT THE UTICA STATE HOSPITAL, UTICA, N. Y.
MADE BY THE W. S. HILL ELECTRIC CO.

concern moved to the present central store, 132 Union Street in April, 1892. The business increased rapidly, and in order to provide for the growing trade a second store was opened September 15, 1893, at 138 Blackmer Street in the south part of the city. The third store was opened October 1, 1895, at 937 Acushnet avenue in the north part of the city. By these three stores customers in the main sections of the city are well accommodated.

The aim of the company has always been to supply the best goods the market affords at honest prices. *All sales are strictly for cash, and no goods are delivered.* By adhering to these two principles it is quite evident that the company can readily sell cheaper than competitors who give credit and employ men and wagons in delivering goods, because by this means bad debts are avoided, and the fixed charges of conducting the business are greatly lessened. By placing the stores in different sections of the city as the company has done, customers from any section of the city are enabled to deal with this concern and carry home their own purchases without undue exertion. The large patronage the company enjoys demonstrates that the people appreciate its methods.

A full line of meats, groceries and provisions is carried in the three stores. Owing to the fact the company has such a large output it is able to buy meats and groceries in car load lots at very advantageous prices, with the result that the goods can thereby be sold at an inside price to the retail trade.

The business was originally managed by W. S. Gordon, who soon after starting it took in as partner, A. G. Hodgdon. The concern is now conducted under the style of the Boston Beef Co., Hodgdon & Gordon, managers and proprietors. Mr. Gordon has had an experience of twenty years and Mr. Hodgdon about fifteen in this line of business, and they are both capable, energetic and wide awake men.

BOSTON BEEF CO.'S STORES.

William F. Nye.

William F. Nye as a manufacturer of sperm, whale and fish oils, and dealer in all the lubricating oils from petroleum, commands a far reaching trade, and in connection with his extensive department for bottling the finer grades of oil for watches, clocks, typewriters, bicycles and sewing machines, his business may be classed as the most unique oil business extant, as by long and continuous advertising he has placed his goods in every leading business centre of the globe. His reputation has become world-wide, and his name a household word among the vast fraternity of watch

WILLIAM F. NYE.

any draft, may be considered one of the finest and the leading oil factory of the country, when the variety and quality of his oils are considered. Mr. Nye has brought this business to its present proportions by a long and almost unparalleled industry, now exceeding thirty years.

Familiar as he was and somewhat identified with the whaling business, since he migrated from among the fishermen of Cape Cod in 1841, to make New Bedford his permanent home, he, at the close of a three years' service in the war of the rebellion, in 1865, engaged in sperm and whale oils exclusively; but ere long it was self evident to him that petroleum was coming to the front as the oil for nearly all purposes, and especially for lubricating the machinery of the world's rapidly increasing industries, and the sequel of his forethought is its introduction by him over the civilized world, under the brands of Machinery Oil, Spindle Oil, Cylinder Oil, Engine Oil, Dynamo Oil, Loom Oil, Standard Axle Oil, etc., each adapted to its purpose as to its fire test, cold test, specific gravity and viscosity.

Perhaps in no one department has he won greater laurels, than with his "Jaw" and "Melon" oils of the blackfish and porpoise. With this oil he stands sponsor for the Horological trade of the world, as he holds the greater portion of the world's supply, and in conjunction with Mr. John Wing, who succeeded to the mana-

and clock makers, sewing machine dealers and bicycle riders. His large stone factory, situated on the immediate water front of the city, accessible by vessels of

WILLIAM F. NYE'S OIL WORKS, FISH ISLAND, NEW BEDFORD.

DENISON, PLUMMER CO., SOUTH MILL, SOUTH WATER STREET.

patented by Mr. J. K. Nye.

The three floors of his factory are most completely arranged, and supplied with hoisting engines and force pumps, tanks and apparatus for refining his many grades of lubricating oils.

Mr. Nye's papers on the food and growth of deep sea fish, and the products and manufacture of their oils, recently read before the Parson's Horological Schools at Peoria, Ill., and La Porte, Ind., are most unique and interesting papers, and afford valuable information to inventors of the many delicately constructed mechanisms of our times, as electrical appliances, locomotive speed recorders, tower clocks, etc., etc.

facture of the Ezra Kelley Oil, uniform prices are established for this rare product.

His typewriter and bicycle oils are especially fine oils, that have met with a sale no less rapid than the introduction of the two machines themselves.

The consumption of bottles by Mr. Nye in his several departments gives employment to some twenty workmen in one of Pittsburg's Flint Glass Factories, and he employs quite the same number of hands, male and female, in his New Bedford factory, filling, corking, packing, and shipping 1,000 gross of these bottles monthly. Frequently in busy seasons, 200 gross of these bottles are filled in a single day, the filling being done in trays of one gross each, in the space of two minutes for each gross, under a patent "Filler," the invention of Mr. J. K. Nye, son of the proprietor, and the corking most effectively and rapidly done by a very simple device, also

The Denison, Plummer Company.

The business carried on by the Denison, Plummer Co., in handling flour and grain is five times larger than that of any other concern in New Bedford and vicinity. Established over thirty years ago, and for a long period a manufacturing house -- converting grain into

DENISON, PLUMMER CO., NORTH BRANCH.

flour and meal—as well as as an extensive dealer in these commodities, the company has discontinued the milling part of the business and greatly enlarged the mercantile department. The present name, the Denison, Plummer Co., was adopted May 1, 1896, and succeeded Denison Bros. Co. In the spring of 1897 all the interests of the Denisons in the company were retired, and the control of the business came into the hands of Henry M. Plummer, who was elected president and treasurer. Mr. Plummer's experience as a practical poultry farmer in the town of Dartmouth admirably fits him to successfully carry on this large hay and grain trade, as he is a skilled judge in regard to grains and the necessities found indispensable by poultry keepers.

The company is now agent for the most reliable brands of flour in the country, including Pillsbury's Best, "Washburn's Best," Cream White, Snow White, and it handles large quantities of its own private brands, the "Eureka" and "Our Best," the excellence of which has been tested for over 25 years by customers in this vicinity and elsewhere. Two places of business are maintained, both of which have within the past few months been extensively enlarged to accommodate the continued increase in the volume of business since Mr. Plummer assumed the management. All customers from the southern portion of the city and the adjacent towns of Dartmouth and Westport will find it most convenient to transact their business at the south mill, so-called, corner of School and Water streets, while those living at the north end or in Acushnet, will find every accommodation at the north branch, 748 Purchase street, which has lately been equipped with a new elevator for discharging grain direct from cars, while increased space has likewise been provided for loading teams.

In these days when so much production that is not standard is put on the market, customers feel that the established reputation of a house is a guarantee of

excellence and reliability. Such is emphatically the case with the Denison, Plummer Co. The trade of the house extends to all the surrounding territory and the facilities for filling all orders however large are unsurpassed by any other establishment in Southeastern Massachusetts, and those entering into business relations with the company may rest assured of receiving such treatment as is in accord with the long established reputation.

Davis & Hatch Spice Co.

The only concern, engaged in the grinding of spices, cream of tartar, and roasting coffee, in New Bedford, or indeed in Southern Massachusetts, with one exception, is the Davis & Hatch Spice Co., whose store and factory is at 28 Union street. The business was started in 1865 on High street by Timothy Davis and Thatcher C. Hatch, under the firm name of Davis & Hatch. About 1887 the concern moved to the present location, and in December, 1893, Mr. Frank E. Fowler purchased the business, and is now sole owner and manager. Under Mr. Fowler's control the business has been prosperous.

The mill where the grinding and manufactur-

DAVIS & HATCH SPICE CO. BUILDING.
No. 28 Union Street.

ing of the spices is carried on is in the rear of the store, and is fitted up with all the modern conveniences and up-to-date machinery used in this manufacture. All the ordinary spices are here prepared and put up in convenient form for the market. The company also deals in teas and coffees, and manufactures and puts up extracts, baking powder, cream of tartar, saleratus, ammonia, blueing, witch hazel, bay rum, insect powder, etc. One of the chief specialties handled is Hatch's Non-Alcoholic Crystal Ginger, put up in tin cans in a dry form, which has proved very popular. All goods are guaranteed to be as represented, and prices are as low as any quoted, considering quality.

7-W

Norman P. Hayes.

Among the leading retail business establishments in New Bedford is the hardware store of Norman P. Hayes, on the corner of William street and Acushnet avenue. Mr. Hayes came to New Bedford in 1879, and started in business at his present location. He was exceedingly fortunate at the outset in his choice of locations, and there are few more eligible sites for business purposes in the city. The structure occupied by him the Andrews building opposite the

erally than New Bedford, and the success of such establishments as Mr. Hayes' is ample proof of this.

Probably one of the most successful patriotic demonstration of a public character ever made under private auspices in this city occurred on Tuesday evening, May 22, 1804, when Mr. Hayes, with the assistance of the Grand Army, Sons of Veterans, etc., caused to be thrown to the breeze a magnificient and costly American flag. The event took place at his business block corner of William street and Acushnet

The Pairpoint Mfg. Co.

While youngest in the galaxy of reputable silverware manufacturers, the Pairpoint Manufacturing Company, of New Bedford, Mass., has made rapid and permanent growth, attaining a marked degree of excellence during the seventeen years since its inception. In 1869, the Mt. Washington Glass Works, now a part of the Pairpoint plant, and started originally at South Boston in 1837, was brought to New Bedford and located on the line of what is now Prospect street. In 1880 the Pairpoint Manufacturing Company was organized, a three story building erected and with power from the Mt. Washington Glass Company (which was really the parent institution) operations were commenced.

Although the ground area was only 120 x 40 feet thing that will give an adequate conception of the splendid display of manufactured products constantly on exhibition at the factory showrooms located at the foot of Howland street. Even then it is hard to realize that under the same spacious roof sand and lead are being skillfully mixed, melted and wrought into the sparkling punch bowl or charming bit of cut tableware, that the dull, crude metals of mother earth are under the masterful hand of the artificer being transformed into rich table furnishings, toilet articles and a thousand and one useful and novel pieces.

People generally are interested in brief descriptions of mechanical processes when accompanied, as everything in these times must be, by illustrations. Take the making of a choice Tea Set, like this one shown

Pairpoint Mfg. Co.

WORKS AT

New Bedford,

MASS.

and the space necessarily limited, a complete line of staple and fancy articles in plate was produced and placed upon the market.

Orders came in rapidly, and then began that sequence of improvements and developments which year by year made the addition of new buildings imperative, until consolidation with the Mt. Washington Glass Works in 1894 the floor area was then equivalent to an avenue 40 feet wide and one mile in length. To carry out this conception we must imagine that along either side of this extended "plaisance" would be ranged skilled workmen, delicate and special machinery, ponderous presses, melting pots and everything in short required to work and mould the crude materials into forms of beauty and utility. The detail of any great institution is invariably beggared by description and a visit to the Pairpoint Works is the only herewith. Block tin, copper, antimony and other materials are carefully melted in certain proportions, and the mixture cast into oblong plates, which are

rolled down to the required thickness, cut into shape and spun into bodies and covers. By a curious method the handles and spouts are cast hollow. The

of these is always interesting to the visitor, and it is generally a surprise to find that even the plainest pieces must pass through so many hands before they reach the jeweler. Heavy drop hammers are used in shaping up the hard metal as the base is largely nickle silver. This class of article is plated by weight and hand finished.

Unquestionably, the finest studios for the hand decoration of fine china and procelain are located at the Pairpoint Works.

To be able to offer genuine *French china* to the American public, and at the same time give them a better class of work and more pleasing style of decoration we have our china blanks made in Limoges, France, to the models which we furnish. Color, that is in the harmonious blending of it, is a source of greater delight probably than any other art. A walk through the Pairpoint Company's ateliers is certainly a feast to the eye. The character of the work is such, however, that visitors cannot at all times be admitted. It is a fact that in decorating, the greatest perfection is reached where the outline of a piece and the decoration harmonize. One of the many advantages of this great concern is therefore apparent, as the decorator can stand by the glass maker and artistic taste and mechanical skill unite in producing a result impossible to each without the other.

The outside equipment is a department of itself. Numbers of "missionaries of commerce" are on the field visiting cities and towns

parts are then assembled and soldered together. By successive handlings the set is polished, plated, burnished by hand and comes out a perfect beauty, rivaling the finest sterling silver.

As glass can only be shaped when exceedingly hot, machinery plays no part in its working. From native Berkshire Hills, sand, skillfully mixed and melted with lead, potash, manganese and other ingredients, we obtain that most useful of metals, namely, glass. The working tools of the glass maker are necessarily few and simple, the plastic mass being largely worked by blowing.

The visitor is usually surprised to see hot glass trimmed off with ordinary scissors when a piece is a little long. The glass maker's is certanly a curious art.

What we are pleased to call *cut glass* is really *polished* glass. The circumference of a bowl for instance is spaced off with a few lines of red paint as a guide and the cutter begins by grinding out these lines on an iron wheel, upon the edge of which a small stream of sand and water is constantly running. This does the cutting and leaves the surface so rough a match can be struck upon it. From this point the pattern is elaborated, finer and finer is the polish until it comes out fit to adorn the lordliest table.

In the line of table furnishings outside the necessary adjunct of spoons, forks and knives, the present social order demands an endless variety of servers, ladles and individual pieces. The manufacture

HISTORY OF THE COMPANY.—The Pairpoint Company was organized in 1880, with Edward D. Mandell as president, Alexander H. Seabury as treasurer, and T. J. Pairpoint as superintendent. The capital stock was originally $100,000, but in July, 1887, it was increased to $400,000, and to $1,000,000 in 1896. Mr. Pairpoint resigned as superintendent April 1, 1885, and was succeeded by Thomas A. Tripp. Mr. Seabury resigned as treasurer in May, 1885, and Mr. Tripp also succeeded him. The present officers are: President, Clarence A. Cook; treasurer and general manager, Thomas

in every State and Territory, together with the Canadian Provinces. For the convenience of buyers visiting the great trade centres, salesrooms are maintained in New York, Chicago, San Francisco and Montreal.

The number of people finding employment with the Pairpoint Company is from nine hundred to one thousand, and ranked with the great majority of industries the average in point of skill and artistic ability runs high.

A word regarding the factory *show rooms.* Here is an elegantly appointed department containing twenty-six hundred square feet of floor space devoted entirely to the display of manufactured products. Brilliant cut glass chandeliers of the company's own make ornament the ceiling, electrical effects bring out the coloring of lamp globes, and numerous unique devices and arrangements gives the place a charming interest to visitors who are always welcome. Articles are for sale as well as display, and by applying at the cashier's desk permits to inspect the Glass Blowing Department may be obtained.

Visitors from out of town cannot spend an hour more pleasantly than by visiting this attractive place, where we can assure them most polite attention. Certainly, the residents of New Bedford should never miss an opportunity of taking friends to see the imposing display of one of the foremost of the city's industries. The factory is located at the foot of Howland street, easily reached via Fourth-street car line.

A. Tripp. The business of the Mount Washington Glass Company was originally started in 1837 at a factory built in South Boston by Deming Jarves, then agent of the Boston & Sandwich Glass Company, and the business was conducted by Capt. Russell. After many changes in owners, the business was in 1869 transferred by W. L. Libbey, then the owner, to the present works on Prospect street, in New Bedford, which had been built by the New Bedford Glass Company. This latter company had but a short existence, owing to financial difficulties. The business was incorporated as the Mt. Washington Glass Company in 1871. In 1894 it was merged in the Pairpoint Manufacturing Company.

The Pairpoint Manufacturing Company employs from nine hundred to one thousand hands, and has many salesmen traveling in different parts of the country. It has a very large export trade. Nearly all the men are expert mechanics, and hundreds of young men from the schools of New Bedford have learned trades in this factory and become proficient workmen. Many of them now hold positions of responsibility, and others have developed into artistic designers and decorators,

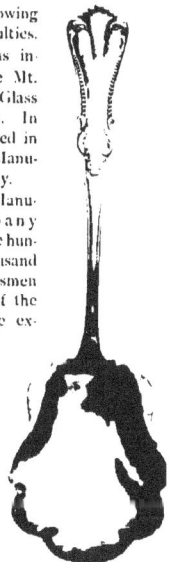

Albert W. Holmes.

The extensive coal business now conducted by Albert W. Holmes on Atlantic wharf foot of Cannon St., was started about 1855 by Joseph Cundall who then erected the wharf. Joseph Cundall was succeeded by Peleg S. Macy, who carried on the business until 1860, when he was succeed by Josiah Holmes, Jr. In 1884, he was succeeded by his son, Albert W. Holmes, who has since then conducted the business. Under the control of the latter the business has increased to large proportions.

The premises occupied have an area of over an acre and a half, where the coal is unloaded by modern

tains an office at 224 Purchase street. From twenty to thirty men are constantly employed.

Mr. Holmes is a native of Mattapoisett, but has resided in New Bedford since his father purchased this business. He is a good example of the best type of conscientious and honorable business men.

Charles M. Comey, formerly a dry goods dealer at the North End, is bookkeeper and clerk for Mr. Holmes, and by his geniality and bonhomie holds many customers.

F. S. Brightman.

For two generations the store at 125, 127 and 129 Union Street has been known as headquarters for

A. W. HOLMES' COAL YARD AND DOCK, ATLANTIC WHARF.

appliances. All coal received comes in barges or schooners, which find convenient dockage here. They are quickly unloaded and the coal transferred to sheds by overhead barrows. The sheds for storing coal are ranged on both sides of the wharf and are quite extensive. On the north side they are five hundred feet long by 50 feet wide, and were built in 1888. On the south side they are 350 feet long by 45 feet wide, erected in 1893. The capacity of the sheds is over 10,000 tons.

Most of the coal received is anthracite, and the trade is chiefly with families. The office at the wharf is convenient for customers residing in the south and central parts of the city, but for the accommodation of his customers at the North End, Mr. Holmes main-

stationery and blank books. That business is still carried on there, although in a more special way made necessary by changing conditions, and is now owned and controlled by Mr. F. S. Brightman, a young man of foresight and ability who, after serving as clerk with Edwin Dews for twelve years, succeeded him in 1893.

Here he conducts a jobbing stationery business, both wholesale and retail, dealing in commercial stationery, blank books, office supplies, paper bags, twines and wrapping papers. He makes a specialty of supplying mills with the goods they demand in his line, and in this department has developed a large trade throughout Southern New England. By giving his personal attention to all details Mr. Brightman has made a pronounced success. He is his own commercial traveler, and his route takes him all over Southeastern Massachusetts, where the bulk of his trade comes from. In addition to his regular business, Mr. Brightman is sole agent in New Bedford and vicinity for the Boston Sunday Herald and Sunday Globe, and has handled on one day as many as 7,000 of those newspapers. His establishment, including the wholesale and retail departments, and the storage rooms, occupies three stories of a large frame building.

William F. Potter & Co.

A leading firm in the wholesale grocery line in New Bedford is that of Wm. F. Potter & Co. The head of the business, Mr. Wm. F. Potter is a native of New Bedford. He was a pupil of the High School in the days of John F. Emerson, and early in life went into the grocery business in the employ of Wood & Brownell, on Union street. From 1853 to 1861, he was a clerk for this concern, and from 1861 to 1865 was a partner in same house.

F. S. BRIGHTMAN'S STATIONERY STORE, 127-129 UNION STREET.

WM. F. POTTER & CO.'S WHOLESALE GROCERY ESTABLISHMENT,
Corner Union and North Front Streets.

In 1865 he severed his connection with Wood & Brownell, and went into the wholesale produce business opposite his present quarters, where he remained until the spring of 1868, when he branched out as a wholesale grocer (handling considerable petroleum oil) at his present location corner of Union and Front streets, which had been previously occupied by W. F. Drown in the same line of business.

The firm with their efficient help and popular salesmen endeavor to please their customers in prices, accommodation and honorable dealing, and point to their past record as a guarantee of its like continuance in the future. The building, Nos. 9, 11, 13 and 15 Union street, which houses the extensive business, is well adapted to its purpose, affording every facility and convenience for the display and accommodation of the large stock carried. The dimensions of the building are 45 by 110 feet, three stories high and its equipment is admirable. Seven hands are employed and two wide-awake travelers represent the firm on the road. The transportation facilities are of the best as the railroad passes the end of the building, while the docks of the New York and of the Martha's Vineyard steamers close by, afford excellent opportunity for receiving and delivering goods.

SPECIMEN OF THE A. L. BLACKMER CO.'S CUT GLASS.

The A. L. Blackmer Company.

The A. L. Blackmer Co., manufacturers of strictly high-grade cut glass, No. 109 North Second street, go to make up one of the many interesting and progressive industries of New Bedford. Starting but a few years ago, this corporation has, in a comparatively short time, by the excellency and high standard of its product, taken a position in the first ranks of the glass-cutting establishments of the country. The motto of its management is to excel in turning out the richest and most elaborate designs and articles that skilled labor can produce in cut glass. That this policy is a good one, one can readily see by looking at the rapid growth of the company and the quantity of its goods, which are to be found in the higher grade art stores in the leading cities of our country.

Several of its designs which are especially worthy of more than casual notice are the "Constellation," which is illustrated on a mammoth footed punch bowl, as shown below; the "Superba," a design new and strikingly original; the "Roman," "Arlington," and many others, all of which are admired for the intricacy of design and the high order of workmanship.

Brett & Simpson.

The old stone building on the cor. of No. Water and Middle Streets, now with many additions, is occupied by Brett & Simpson, Soap and Washing Powder manufacturers, who do the largest business of any like concern in this section.

The old stone building has been standing ever since 1815, at which time John James Howland built it for a candle factory.

OFFICERS OF THE NEW BEDFORD INSTITUTION FOR SAVINGS FROM THE BEGINNING UNTIL THE PRESENT. Presidents: William Rotch, Jr., Abraham Barker, Thomas Mandell, Pardon Tillinghast, William C. Taber, William Watkins and William W. Crapo who was elected in 1896. Treasurers--Abraham Shearman. Jr., William C. Taber, George W. Baker, William C. Taber (treasurer, pro tem.), Reuben Nye, William C. Coffin and Charles H. Pierce who has served since 1870.

From the beginning of its career the institution has prospered constantly. In 1830 the funds amounted to $160,477.95; in 1840 to $240,298.37; in 1850 to $577,448.01; in 1860 to $2,070,395.80; in 1870 to $5,436,263.60; in 1880 to $8,835,984.62; in 1890 to $11,540,767.24 and on July 17th, to $13,412,226.57.

The Philadelphia & Reading Coal and Iron Co.

Ranking among the largest plants for receiving and distributing coal on the Atlantic seaboard, are the extensive coal pockets of the Philadelphia &

The premises are at the foot of Walnut street, and occupy an area of 6.14 acres.

The plant was established and the main pocket on the wharf erected in 1873 by the Philadelphia &

leased to various firms until 1882, when the owners
took possession, and proceeded to utilize the plant
as a forwarding and distributing depot for the company's coals to the local mills, and to inland dealers
and manufacturers. The latter traffic is carried on
by means of the cars of the Old Colony Railroad
Company to all points on its main branches and connections. Since the company took control of the
property the business has assumed immense proportions.

The entire plant consists of a main pocket, on the
end of the wharf, 210 feet long, forty feet wide and
forty-five feet high, with a capacity of 7,200 tons;
a shipping pocket, 100 feet long, at the head of the
north side of the dock; and fourteen immense bins,
connected with the shipping pocket, into which the

York Harbor, at which points it is received direct by
cars from the company's mines in Pennsylvania. A
number of vessels can be discharged at once as the
property has 2210 feet of wharf line, in front of
which is sufficient water for the largest crafts that
come in.

The fourteen storage bins are situated at the head
fo the wharf and occupy a space extending to South
Water street. On a portion of the area they cover, the
New Bedford Marine Railway was formerly located.
The bins have a total capacity of 130,000 tons, and are
intended for the storage of the winter's supply of
coal during the ice embargo, when the weather
renders uncertain the arrival of cargoes. The bins
are of a peculiar but very effective construction. The
sides are formed of triangles of heavy timbers, twenty-
six feet high, the outer edge inclined at about an angle
of seventy-five degrees, and the base resting on the
ground. They are strongly braced, are placed five feet
apart, and connected on the outside with heavy 3-inch
planks which forms the walls of the bins. No posts are
sunk in the ground. When coal is put in these bins the
triangles act on the principle of the truss, and the greater the load, within certain limits, the stronger the bins
are. The coal is sometimes heaped

BLOSSOM BROS.' PLANING MILL, 172 NORTH WATER STREET.

coal is conducted by overhead runways and stored
until needed. Railroad tracks traverse the entire
area, extending to and passing underneath and along-
side the shipping and main pockets, and encircling
the mammoth bins, so that every one can be tapped
directly by the cars.

Most of the coal is now brought in by large barges
or schooners, and some of it in iron steamers. Vessels
of twenty-one feet draft can come up to either the
main or the shipping pocket, and the cargoes the
barges and schooners now bring range from 2,300 to
3,000 tons. The company's large steamers and barges
can be discharged with the appliances now in use by
unloading from four hatches at once, in about 8 hours.
steamer "Pottsville," with 1,750 tons, was unloaded in
7 1-2 hours. The coal received in New Bedford comes
from the company's own depots at Port Richmond on
the Delaware, or Port Reading on Staten Island, New

up twenty-five feet above the edges of the storage
bins. Attached to the storage bins are shipping bins
provided with shoots to discharge coal into the cars,
at an elevation to provide screening.

At the harbor end of the bins is a boiler house,
containing three boilers, two of sixty horse power
each and one of forty-five, which furnish steam for
eleven hoisting engines and derricks, and for a winch
on the wharf for hauling cars, and also for heating
purposes. When vessels are being unloaded from 100
to 150 men are employed.

A few statistics compiled from the company's
books will give an idea of the extent of the business:

Largest year 1894 output on N. Y., N. H. & H. R. R. cars
204,504 4-20 tons.

Largest month of same September, 1894 36,800 11-20 tons.

Week ending June 15, 1894, as per pay roll, 13,384 tons discharged
from vessels.

30 working days, after October 2, 1893—16,260 tons discharged from vessels.

Largest week's car service, January 23-28, 1893— 1,682 cars; April 11–17, 1893 1,548 cars; Sept. 17–21, 1896, 1,534 cars.

Schooner " Saganore," 2,214 tons, arrived 6 a. m. March 13, 1895; discharged 12 m. March 14, 1895; 13 working hours, all on cars, is an instance of quick work.

The business of the company is altogether whole-sale, and it does not consequently come into compe-tition with the local dealers. It however, gives employment to many persons in the city, and furnishes a large amount of business to the railroad. In view of these facts it would be a very short-sighted policy for the New Bedford city fathers to do anything that would operate against the business of the company. The raising of the railroad tracks, in order to avoid a grade crossing at the approach to the new bridge, as has been proposed, and evidently favored by the City Council in 1893, would certainly have this effect, as such an elevation would be a permanent blockade on account of the heavy grades, or necessitate the elevation of the whole plant of the company. The great expense would preclude the company accepting the latter alternative, as it would probably prefer, under such conditions, to remove its plant elsewhere.

Charles W. Agard is the local superintendent in New Bedford, and the business has been developed to a large extent under his management.

Blossom Brothers.

The firm of Blossom Brothers operate an extensive planing mill at 172 North Water street, and are man-ufacturers and dealers in window and door frames, sash and blinds. The factory was constructed with special reference to the details of the manufacture, and the equipment of machinery and appliances are of the most modern and improved character. The entire plant covers an area of about an acre. On the premises is a dry house of the most improved pattern.

They have recently added a nice moulding machine, which affords them special facilities for the manufac-ture of mouldings and fine interior finish, and they are now leaders in the production of special mouldings. The firm now makes a specialty of plate and window glass, of which a large stock is constantly carried, and great care is exercised in putting in glass anywhere when ordered. A force of 25 expert men in the various departments of the industry is constantly employed. Special attention given to wood turning, in which they excel, both in artistic finish and dura-bility of the work. Sawing and planing and general jobbing is promptly attended to. The partnership was entered into in 1889 by S. J. and Charles Blossom, and the business has been one of expansion ever since, every year witnessing an increased output.

David Duff & Son.

The coal business now conducted by David Duff & Son (David and John Duff) is the oldest in its line in New Bedford. It was originally established by a man named Crane. He was succeeded by Captain George Randall, who was followed by E. P. Haskell. The latter was succeeded by Parker & Haskell.

The business was purchased from Parker & Haskell

WHARVES OF DAVID DUFF & SON, FISH ISLAND, NEW BEDFORD

Coal Piers, Elevators and Sheds for Storing Coal.

by David Duff & Son, June 1, 1887. From the beginning under the management of the new firm, the trade rapidly increased and it was soon found necessary to enlarge the old quarters on Fish Island. The original sheds on the south side of the bridge and east side of the island were enlarged until now they have a capacity of about 5,000 tons. A new pocket was erected 112 by 38 feet in area, with a height of 21 feet between the floor and the run. This pocket is provided with a hoisting apparatus of an improved pattern, and it has a capacity of 3,000 tons. The firm now handles over 50,000 tons annually, over ten times the amount that was handled when the business was purchased ten years ago.

In 1893 the firm purchased property on the north

Indeed this was the original business of the firm, in which line Mr. David Duff started in 1868, on Acushnet avenue, north of Maxfield street. Afterward the headquarters were transferred to Front street, to a building which occupied the present site of Armour & Co.'s new packing house. All sorts of general and heavy teaming and cartage is done. Safes and other heavy materials are moved, and a great deal of work is done for the mills and large corporations.

The main office of the firm is in the basement of the Five Cent Saving bank, 37 Purchase street, a branch office is maintained at the North End in the Wamsutta block, 669 Purchase street; and there is also an office at the coal yards on Fish Island. The

GREENE & WOOD RECEIVING DOCKS.

side of the bridge, extending to the west side of the island, where there is excellent whartage. Here an extensive run was erected to unload bituminous coal, brought in for the use of the cotton mills. A considerable business is now done in this line, and the soft coal brought in here is at once carted to customers, so that very little storage facilities are needed. The entire area in both yards amounts to about five and a half acres, a much larger space than is occupied by any other local coal dealer. The wharf lines of the entire property on both sides of the island measure 1,237 feet, and the coal is brought in by large barges and schooners. A new stable and shed was built on the north side in 1896, and has accommodation for 70 horses, which are all used by the firm in the different departments of the business.

David Duff & Son also do a large teaming business.

office for the teaming business is at 60 Front street. Mr. John Duff is now the active manager of the business.

Greene & Wood.

The oldest and the most extensive lumber business in the city of New Bedford is that conducted by Greene & Wood. The firm not only deals in lumber but also operates a planing and wood working mill.

The business dates back to the middle of the century, having been started by Samuel Leonard in 1835, at the east side of Clark's Cove, near the present bathhouses. For many years all the timber was brought up into the cove and rafted ashore. A few years later Mr. Leonard built the present Leonard's wharf, removed the business there, where it has continued since. At the time of the removal to the new location, Samuel Leonard's son, Henry T. Leonard, took the business, forming a partnership with Augustus A. Greene, a prominent young carpenter who had come here from Providence to build the houses now owned by the estates of Abraham H. Howland, Miss Julia Delano and Frederick Grinnell.

Under the firm style of Leonard & Greene, the business was continued until 1848, when Henry T.

GREENE & WOOD —PLANING MILL.

plete assortment of building lumber is kept on hand constantly, and this requires a large area of land to sort it and pile it conveniently for customers. This concern is the only one in the city dealing in southern pitch pine timber, plank, and boards, which the firm lands on its wharf direct from the south in vessels. Several large storage buildings contain the finished lumber and hard woods. The illustrations give a general idea of the premises.

As the years have passed the firm has extended its business to meet the changing character of the trade. The planing and wood working mill was burned Aug. 8, 1888, and almost wholly destroyed, but was immediately rebuilt on a much larger scale, and fitted with the newest machinery and best appli-

GREENE & WOOD —HARD PINE YARD.

Wood bought out Henry T. Leonard, and the style of the firm became Greene & Wood. Under this name it has remained for nearly fifty years, and in one location has carried on the business with success. Next year will consequently be the semi-centennial of the firm of Greene & Wood. Mr. Greene retired in 1872 and Henry T. Wood died in 1883. The present firm consists of William G. Wood, who entered it in 1861, and George R. Wood and Edmund Wood, who were admitted soon after the death of their father in 1883. The firm now owns and occupies nine acres of land on the water front, including a wharf, and the entire area is utilized in the business. A com-

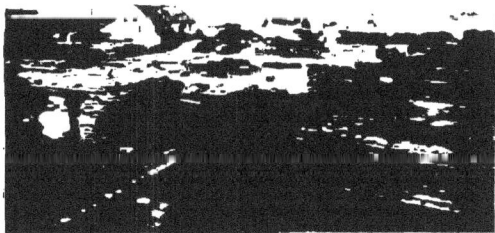

ances for fine and accurate work. It occupies an area of 120 by 138 feet, two stories high, and is admirably adapted for handling lumber rapidly and economically. The dry kiln is a separate building 40 by 80 feet, two stories high. Here the Sturtevant hot blast drying process is employed, with a separate engine. Both these new buildings are well protected against fire by Grinnell automatic sprinklers and other appliances used by our cotton mills. In this mill all kinds of planing, sawing and turning are done, some very heavy machines being employed. The firm now employs forty men.

Stephen C. Lowe.

A man whose career is representative of the great changes that have taken place in the industrial and social conditions of New Bedford is Stephen C. Lowe. He has achieved very marked success, without any

OIL CAN.

other aid than his own energy and ability. Coming to New Bedford from England with his parents in his early childhood, in his boyhood he worked in the Wamsutta Mills for years. As he grew up, not finding the scope in the cotton mills for the energy he possessed, he engaged in various occupations. In 1875 he went to Montreal, Canada, where he had some relatives, and obtained a situation in a large house-furnishing concern. Here he remained two years and

obtained a good knowledge of business affairs and practical details. Returning to New Bedford he became the active manager of a stove and house-furnishing store in connection with which there was a plumbing and tinsmith business. In this situation he obtained a wide and varied experience, and had an opportunity to exercise and develop his business talents for management and organization.

Leaving this position, he started in 1883, at 635 Purchase street, a house-furnishing store, dealing in stoves, ranges, etc., and he also carried on plumbing and tinsmithing. For years he had a hard struggle, but by stern application and persistence he slowly obtained a more substantial foothold. In 1889 and 1890 he enlarged his business by adding to it a line of mill supplies and furnishings of all kind, and this department increased on his hands to such an extent that it rapidly became the main portion of his business. He established shops in the rear of his store and engaged in the manufacture of a number of specialties.

Finally the manufacturing branch of his business increased to such an extent that larger and more centrally located quarters were needed. To provide such Mr. Lowe purchased the large three story frame building, Nos. 87 to 91 Union street, so long occupied by the offices and plant of the New Bedford *Standard.* Here he transferred his manufacturing, plumbing and tinsmithing and mill supply business in June 1895. The ground floor is occupied by the office and salesrooms, and in the rear are storerooms. The two upper floors are devoted to manufacturing, the main workroom being on the second floor, and the shops are equipped with the most modern machinery necessary in the manufacture.

A number of valuable specialties are manufactured, and Mr. Lowe owes his success chiefly to their excellence and the skill and thoroughness with which they are fashioned. Chief among these are the " Needling Combers," an English invention for use in the manipulation of cotton for the production of fine yarns, and which have come into wide use in New Bedford since the great increase in the spinning mills. Mr. Lowe equipped his shops with tools from England and went into the production of these combers extensively. They are known as the Heatherington, Dobson & Barlow Combs. He imports the fine needles from England by the million. The excellence of the work on these combers is such that Mr. Lowe not only supplies the city mills, but receives orders from all over New England, and from Philadelphia and New York and elsewhere.

Another specialty that has been very popular is an oil cabinet made of galvanized sheet iron, with only one seam ; it is iron bound, strong and durable, with no liability to leakage and has been very popular in the local mills. The cabinet was first manufactured at the suggestion of Mr. William J. Kent, of the Wamsutta Mills, and many of the local mills are supplied with them. It is the invention of Mr. Lowe.

Among the other articles of excellence Mr. Lowe manufactures, are cylinders for spinning frames and mules; card screens; oil drippers of original design; comber waste boxes of galvanized iron, by means of which the danger from fire is avoided and space saved as compared with wooden boxes previously in use for this purpose; roving cans; cornices and gutters for buildings, which are made on a large " brake " located on the second story, and which weighs two tons. The manufacturing department is also fitted to repair anything in the mill supply line.

A large stock of supplies is carried, consisting of wrought iron and brass pipe and cast iron pipe, which is kept on the first floor, but on the third floor

land speculation. In 1895 he purchased the Homer estate on County street for $25,000, and sold it the present year for $37,000. He has also been successful in various other land deals.

The French in New Bedford.

New Bedford has a French population of nearly 13,000 souls, divided into three parishes: Sacred Heart established in 1870; St. Hyacinthe in 1888 and St. Antoine in 1895. Each of these parishes has a large and well equipped school, giving instruction yearly to 1,300 children. There is an asylum for young children whose mothers work in the mills. This asylum is also equipped as a kindergarden.

Fifty years ago there was not a French resident in

SPECIALTIES MANUFACTURED BY S. C. LOWE, 87 TO 91 UNION STREET.

a full line of crockery, tanks, seats, and all sorts of fittings necessary for an extensive plumbing business are stored. These goods Mr. Low purchases by the car loads. For use in the mill supply department over 1,000 pounds of tacks are carried in stock.

Mr. Lowe carries a very large stock of belting— single belts from one inch to eight inch, and double belts from two inch to twelve inch; and is the New Bedford agent for the Union Belt Co. of Fall River. For several years he has been agent for the Crawford bicycle, and during the season of 1897 sold 218 wheels. He also pays a great deal of attention to repairing bicycles, and has done a large business in this department. In his entire business, Mr. Lowe employs an average of thirty hands, and his weekly pay roll is $350.

Mr. Lowe's present fortune was not all acquired in his business, but he has made considerable money by

New Bedford. Some came here after the civil war, but they began to come in large numbers about 1870. They have now six benevolent societies of which they are proud, and a daily newspaper "L'Echo du Soir." They are represented in the common council by M. Joseph Magnant and in the banking business by M. Joseph Poisson, who is director of two banks. A great number of the French residents of New Bedford are American citizens, and take an active part in politics. A great number too, are proprietors of houses and land, some of them being quite wealthy. The real estates belonging to French citizens is valued at $902,053.00.

All of the French citizens keep with great care the language and the religion of their fathers, but they nearly all speak English, and are proud to be American citizens. They have amongst them doctors, merchants, justices of the peace, lawyers, overseers of the mills, real estate agents, etc.

J. A. CARON.

H. L. BORDEN.

New Bedford Rubber Co.

The New Bedford Rubber Co., 67 William street, wholesale and retail dealers in rubber goods and

mill supplies, was started in October, 1895, by T. P. Himes, of Providence, who installed his brother, Raymond Himes, as manager. The business was conducted under the above management until June 1, 1897, when it was found necessary to make an assignment. The establishment was purchased of the assignee by the present owner, Harry L. Borden, who had had considerable experience in the line of mill supplies. Under Mr. Borden's management the trade has largely increased, and the company is rapidly attaining a leading position in its own specialties. Two salesmen are constantly employed. One devotes his time to the jobbing drug trade and local trade about the city, and the other sells the mechanical line of rubber goods to mills, shops, factories, steamboats, etc. The company makes a specialty of mackintoshes at reasonable prices, and also of oil cloth garments for seamen. The goods carried consist, in part, of hose, tubing, packing, sheeting, syringes, water bottles, blankets, boots and shoes, oil clothing, toys, policemen's and firemen's coats, etc. The line of mill and factory supplies comprise cotton and linen, unlined and lined hose, suction hose of all kinds, steam hose, fire hose, and garden hose; sheet packing of every description, also flax packing; valves, bunters, and everything else in the rubber line. The company is sole agent and distributor for New Bedford, of the famous Knowlton packings. Special attention is given to the repairing of rubber goods. All goods are guaranteed for a reasonable length of time, and if anything is found defective it is cheerfully made good. The emblem of the company is *Everything in Rubber.*

Gifford & Co.

For many years the firm of Gifford & Co., have been leaders in the business community of New Bedford, and their store has always been a headquarters for first class clothing. The business was started in 1853, by Nathan T. Gifford, and for 41 years was located at 139 Union street, between Acushnet avenue and Second street. In 1894 the concern removed to the present large quarters, No. 22 Pleasant street, in the Masonic building. This is the new and attractive

obtained a certain prestige. Mr. Parker purchased the business about eight years ago, and has conducted it successfully since then.

The dimensions of the present store are 60x46 feet. It is well lighted at the front by large plate glass windows, and at the rear by ordinary windows. By this means excellent light is furnished in every part of the store, which is a great desideratum to customers in picking out goods. The manager of the business is William L. Bly. He was formerly mana

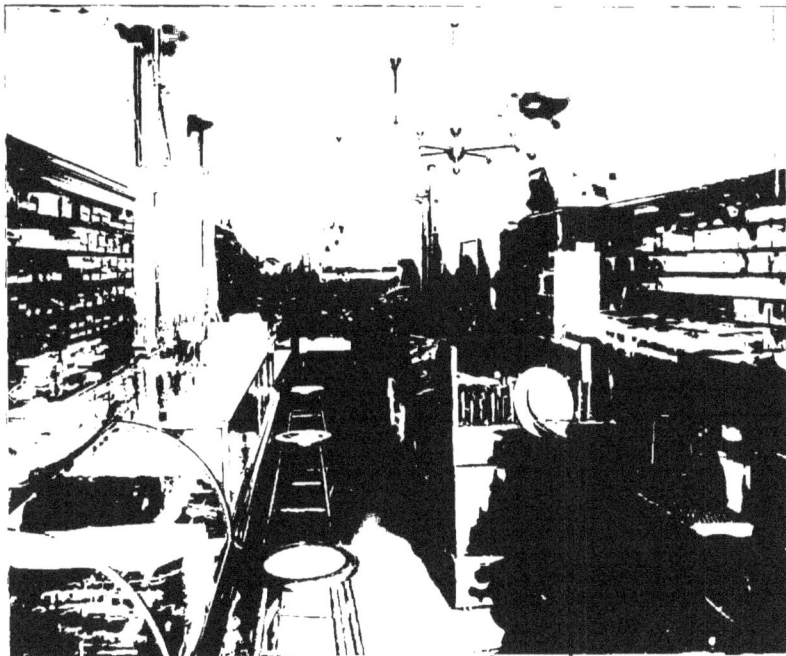

INTERIOR GIFFORD & CO.'S CLOTHING AND GENTS' FURNISHING STORE.
No. 22 Pleasant Street.

retail region of the city, and the store is almost opposite City Hall Park.

The firm carries a full line of men's, boy's and youth's clothing, hats and caps, gentlemen's furnishings, underwear, hosiery and neckwear. The clothing is manufactured by first-class makers, and the firm makes a specialty of the garments made by Shuman & Co., of Boston, one of the largest manufacturers of clothing in the country.

H. W. Parker, a well known citizen, whose family have contributed much to the development of New Bedford, is now the sole owner of the business. He has retained the old name because the business had been conducted under it so many years that it had

ger for three years, and has recently been re-engaged. He has had a lengthy experience in this business, fifteen years in Boston and ten in New Bedford, and is a capable and courteous salesman.

The Pedigree of Mrs. Hetty Green.

Gideon Howland was a member of one of the most celebrated of whaling firms, I. Howland, Jr., & Co. He had two daughters, Sylvia Ann and Abigail. The former died in 1865, leaving a property of about $2,000,000. Abigail married Edward Mott Robinson, and their daughter, Hetty Howland Robinson, married Edward Green, of New York. She is now reputed to be the wealthiest woman in America. Gideon Howland died in 1847. Miss Robinson was the heir to $5,000,000 from her father and $1,000,000 from her aunt.

J. & W. R. Wing & Co.

The firms of J. & W. R. Wing and J. & W. R. Wing & Co. are among the oldest business houses in New Bedford, the firm of J. & W. R. Wing, having been established by Joseph Wing and William R. Wing nearly fifty years ago. The firm of J. & W. R. Wing & Co. was established about thirty years ago, and has always been an extensive dealer in clothing, and at present carries a large stock of the best makes of clothing, hats, caps, and furnishings for men and boys, bicycle clothing, sweaters, shirts, golf hose, tennis and bathing suits, wraps and house coats and gowns, mackintoshes, umbrellas, canes, jewelry, trunks, bags, etc.

The firms occupy a fine three story brick building of their own, Nos. 131 and 133 Union Street. The store has massive plate glass windows and polished oak fixtures. The present members of the firm of J. & W. R. Wing & Co. are William R. Wing and John Wing.

The firm of J. & W. R. Wing conduct a large and important business as managing owners and agents for whaling vessels, and as importers of sperm and whale oils and whalebone.

Charles O. Brightman.

One of the best known and most successful contractors and builders in New Bedford is Charles O.

J. & W. R. WING & CO.'S BUILDING, 131-133 UNION ST.

Brightman, whose office and factory is in the old stone building 72 North Water street, corner of Rodman street. Mr. Brightman established his business in 1879, and has met with a large degree of success. He furnishes plans and estimates for all kinds of buildings, and has the reputation of being an expeditious and careful builder. The extent of his operation and the character of his work can be readily judged from the buildings he has erected, which are his best credentials.

Among the buildings which Mr. Brightman has erected are the following: Wamsutta block, Purchase street; Haskell & Tripp's block of stores; Adelphi Rink, County street; Howland Mills; Rotch Mills, Nos. 1 and 2; Columbia Mills, Nos. 1 and 2; Bennett Mill, No. 2; Lambeth Rope Mill; House of Correction, Union, County and Ash streets; the residences of Charles M.Tripp, Clarence A. Cook, Charles S Kelley, Edmund B. Wood, Frank R. Hadley, Charles M. Hussey, Samuel P. Richmond, John Duff; Episcopal Parish House; Unitarian Parish House; Emerson block, Union and Sixth streets; Union for Good Works building, Market street; Sanford and Kelley's banking house building, Pleasant street; Five Cents Savings Bank building, Purchase street; addition to Parker House; Slocum building, Pur

C. O. BRIGHTMAN'S BUILDING, 72 NORTH WATER STREET.

chase and Middle streets; St. Luke's Hospital building; Madison Street School House and many others in New Bedford; United States Fish Commission building at Woods Holl, Mass.; Globe Yarn Mill, No. 3, Fall River, Mass. Mr. Brightman employs none but competent and faithful workmen.

New York Market.

A meat and general provision store, which from its size, the skill with which the goods are displayed

NEW YORK MARKET, 64 PURCHASE STREET.

in the windows and on the front of the premises, and the cleanness and neatness of all the goods and arrangements, attracts general attention and commendation, is the establishment of the New York Market at 64 Purchase Street. It is directly opposite the Merchants Bank building, and has consequently one of the most central locations in the city.

The store was established Oct. 14, 1892, and will therefore be five years old during the Semi Centennial Celebration. A general line of the very best meats and provisions is kept in stock, including fresh and salt meats, all kinds of fruits and vegetables in their season, and a specialty is made of turkeys, chickens, fowls, and all sorts of poultry. A very large assortment of the best brands of canned goods, including meats, vegetables and fish is constantly carried in stock, and the supply on hand is very tastefully arranged so as to make an attractive and picturesque display when viewed from the street.

The store is noticeably attractive. The fruit and vegetables are displayed at the front in a very inviting way, while everything is kept in an immaculate condition of cleanliness in all parts of the store. Customers are attracted by these character istics, as everything displayed under such conditions looks good to eat. The store is large and roomy, about 30 x 70 feet in dimensions. At the rear is an ice box 14 x 14 feet, which requires twelve tons of ice to maintain a proper temperature. It is fitted with overhead railways from which meat carcasses are suspended and by means of which they can be readily handled. The ice is put in from the rear of the building by a skid. The trade of the store is with the leading hotels, the large boarding houses, and with the best class of families.

The proprietor of the business is E. C. Brownell, who also personally conducts a similar establishment, known as the Fourth Ward Market, corner of Sixth and Market Streets opposite, the City Hall, under the firm name of E. C. Brownell & Co. The New York Market is managed by E. A. Hoxie, who has served in this capacity since it was started. Mr. Hoxie has had sixteen years' experience in this line of business, and he is a very energetic and capable marketman.

C. F. Wing.

The largest department store dealing in carpets, drapery, furniture, crockery, house and kitchen furnishing and specialties, at the present time, not only in New Bedford, but in Southern Massachusetts, is the emporium of C. F. Wing at 34 to 40 Purchase street. The premises are larger and the business greater in its own line than that of any other concern in this region of country outside of Boston. The business was started in a modest way in 1878, in a store which occupied the south half of the old Nathan Chase property, with a stock of dry goods and a small carpet department. The carpet business increased so rapidly, that after a few years, the dry goods department was closed out and the whole store devoted to the carpet trade. This line under the new conditions increased more and more, so that enlarged quarters became necessary, and to accommodate the expanding business, the Wing Building, a three-story brick block, was erected in 1887, at which time departments of wall paper and draperies were added.

The next radical change was made in 1890, when on the second floor of the Wing Building a small stock of furniture was put in, consisting principally of "Odd Pieces," including parlor pieces, fancy chairs,

cabinets, etc. In less than a year this department had increased so rapidly, that a lease of the Waite Building, the next property adjoining the Wing Building on the north, was secured for ten years, and a general line of furniture was at once placed before the public.

Meanwhile the business continued to increase in every department, so that the accommodations in both the Wing and Waite Buildings had become insufficient and inadequate for the trade, making it more and more difficult to attend to the wants of customers. Under these circumstances enlarged quarters were imperatively needed. Accordingly, early in 1897, the Manhattan

C. F. WING PARLOR FURNITURE DEPARTMENT.
Nos. 34 to 40 Purchase Street.

House property, owned by Mr. Michael Kane, was purchased by Mr. Wing, and he immediately began to erect a four story brick building 65 x 88, which occupies all the area in the rear of the Wing Building and Spaulding property, and extends back to Hall's court. With this large addition the premises have a depth of 150 feet from Purchase street to Hall's court, and a width of eighty-eight feet. This arrangement gives ample light both front and back. Between the old and new buildings, but within the limits of the addition, is an oblong well twenty feet long by ten feet wide, extending from the first floor to the roof and surmounted by a glass roof which also aids very materially in furnishing light to every floor of the old and new buildings. The new building is also furnished with excellent Morse electric elevators, both passenger and freight, running from the basement to top story, and the former is located just north of the

C. F. WING   CROCKERY DEPARTMENT.

at which time Mr. Wing will add this space to his establishment. All that will be necessary to bring this into communication with the rest of the store will be to break through the wall on each side of the light well.

The wall paper department, which is a large and flourishing part of the business, is located at the rear end of the first floor of the Waite Building, while the balance of this floor is devoted to chamber suites including brass and iron bedsteads.

An important feature just introduced is a crockery department, which is located on the south side of the first floor of the Wing Building. All grades of tableware are carried. The north side of this floor is devoted to draperies and shades, in which line this store carries the finest stock in this section of the country. A large kitchen furnishing department is also conducted in the Wing Building.

The new building as well as the original Wing Building have been so constructed that they can be carried up several stories higher if the necessities

light well. The building was completed and arranged about October 1st, so that everything is brand new and will well repay a visit at this time.

The first floor of the new building is devoted to parlor furniture. The second is wholly given over to carpets, of which Mr. Wing carries the largest stock and best grades in the city. The third floor is reserved for cabinet furniture, bookcases, desks, and case work of all kinds. The fourth floor is occupied by the upholstery and carpet workrooms, which are fitted with the latest improved appliances used in these branches of work. The basement is devoted partly to storage and partly to a department stocked with oil cloths, linoleums, and other floor coverings of a practical character. All the rooms are connected with the office by telephone.

In the Wing Building, the old part of the store, only two floors are occupied at present. The third floor is used by the Knights of Pythias as a hall, but their lease will expire in July, 1898,

of the business should require it in the future. The new building has a flat roof, and from it can be had one of the best views attainable of the harbor, the bay and the city. The whole water front is in range, and the majority of the great mills are in sight in the distance at either end of the city.

From the beginning of the business Mr. James N. Parker has been with Mr. Wing. At the start he managed the carpet department. He is now the general superintendent and has been a very efficient and faithful aid to Mr. Wing in building up the business. Mr. Ernest A. Jennings has been with the house since 1880. He has charge of the buying in certain lines, and to his labors and energy much of the success of the enterprise is due.

Pope's Island Manufacturing Corporation.

The Pope's Island Manufacturing Corporation takes its name from the island it occupies, which is in the centre of the Acushnet River, midway between New Bedford and Fairhaven, and over which the

to 26 inches. The sheet metal is especially adapted for use where plated metal is used. For drawing, spinning and stamping it is excellent. It makes a very superior line of table ware, is easily worked, takes and retains a magnificent finish, and is very strong. For use in jewelry, ornaments, badges or novelties of any kind, it works easily and requires no plating.

The non-corrosive white metal has a beautiful white color, great strength, and is susceptible of a very high finish. It is malleable and ductile, and can be easily spun or drawn; is superior to German silver and aluminum in its working qualities, and in soldering and brazing it gives no trouble. Its color is about the same as that of coin silver, which is retained by the finished metal without plating.

The non-corrosive white metal is also especially well adapted for harness and carriage trimmings, and for yacht and boat finishings. The corporation makes the only non-corrosive horse bit in the market out of this metal, for which a large trade has been secured all over the United States. The Massachusetts Char-

WORKS OF THE POPE'S ISLAND MANUFACTURING CORPORATION, POPE'S ISLAND.

long bridge, now in process of reconstruction, passes. The corporation was formed in 1891, under a charter from the State of Massachusetts, with a capital stock of $165,000, for the purpose of manufacturing metals, especially non-corrosive metals in sheets, wire, and in special forms and articles.

The foundry and machine shop was erected when the company was organized in 1891. The business increased rapidly, and to keep up with the demand the rolling mill was erected in 1894. It has a capacity of three tons daily. In the works forty-five men, all skilled workmen, are constantly employed. The illustration on this page gives a very good idea of the extent and appearance of the establishment.

The plant produces non-corrosive brass and German silver, and white and bronze metals in sheets, wire, pigs and rods, for which there is a growing demand all over the country. Foundry castings are also made to order. These metals are suitable for spoons, forks, table ware, harness and carriage mountings, yacht and boat trimmings, jewelry, art work and novelties. The white and bronze metals are produced in sheets or rolls, to No. 36 B. & S. gauge, and widths

itable Mechanics Association in 1895 awarded a silver medal to the Pope's Island Manufacturing Corp. for the excellence of their new Metallic Composition for harness trimmings, etc. The phosphor-bronze metal produced is the best composition in the market at present for use in journals or bearings of shafting and machinery. The gold bronze closely imitates gold, its tensile strength is high, its working qualities very good, it is capable of taking and retaining a very high finish, and can be stamped, spun or drawn with greater facility than brass. As a jeweler's metal it is unequalled by anything in the market, both in color and working quality, and is much superior to brass or oroide in its resistance to tarnish and corrosion.

The industry carried on by this corporation is the only one of its kind in this part of the country, and the mill is the only one outside of the combination or trust. The corporation makes a special effort to reach jewelry manufacturers, to supply them with sheet metal and wire, especially the gold bronze, the white metal and the German silver.

The phosphor-bronze which is produced for machinery bearings, is known as "spermoline bearing

E. T. CHAPMAN.

metal," is especially adapted for high speed and heavy work, being hard and tough, and having lubricating qualities superior to anything of the kind in the market.

The president of the Pope's Island Manufacturing Corporation is David B. Kempton. W. O. Sheldon is treasurer and is the active manager of the works and business.

E. T. Chapman.

The oldest cigar and tobacco business in New Bedford is that conducted by E. T. Chapman. His main store is at 66 William street, and a branch store is

big fire which on Feb. 22, 1873, destroyed a number of buildings. The store was then started anew on Second street, between William and Union streets, but was soon moved back to Purchase street where it was located directly opposite the central engine house, in the premises now occupied by Schule Brothers. From there it was removed to the southeast corner of William street and Acushnet avenue, on the site now occupied by the new postoffice, where it remained until the premises had to be vacated in order that the building might be pulled down to make way for the postoffice. At that time, which was in 1887, Mr. Chapman secured his present quarters, southwest corner of William street and Acushnet avenue, where he has an attractive and commodious store. The branch store at 99 1-2 Union street was established in 1891.

Mr. Chapman in his two stores carries the largest stock of cigars and tobacco in the city, including foreign and domestic cigars, and smoking and chewing tobacco. He is the proprietor of several special brands of cigars of excellent quality, among which the best known are "The Firm" and "Plymouth Club," 10 cent cigars; and "Chapman's Star Smoker" and "Seal of New Bedford" 5 cent cigars, and is likewise proprietor of the well known brand of smoking and chewing tobacco "Chapman's 900," which he has sold for fifteen years. The store is also headquarters for J. Wright & Co.'s tobaccos, Lorrillard's, Dills, B. L. Planet, and all the other leading brands. A large variety of all kinds of pipes is constantly carried and

INTERIOR OF E. T. CHAPMAN'S CIGAR STORE.

maintained at 99 1-2 Union street. Mr. Chapman started in business in 1866 on the west side of Purchase street, between Union and William streets, where he remained until he was burned out in the

the display in this department is well worthy of examination by smokers. His line of meerschaums is the most extensive in the city. He also carries on a wholesale business and his delivery wagon is the finest ornamented in the city.

"THE HACIENDA," 923 ACUSHNET AVENUE — NORTH END.

Frank R. Pease.

The Pease Prescription Pharmacy, one of the leading drug stores in the flourishing retail district of the North End, occupies the northwest corner of Cook & Smith's large building, "The Hacienda," 923 Acushnet avenue, corner of Cedar Grove street. It is one of the most complete and elegantly furnished drug stores in the whole city, and was established in this neighborhood ten years ago; the present stand, four years. Mr. Pease, at his North End store, also deals in seeds and carries a full line to select from.

Mr. Pease has been in the druggist business from boyhood, and graduated as a pharmacist under the instruction of his father, William A. Pease, who for many years conducted the apothecary's store in this city on The Hill. After learning his profession he had several years' experience in Boston in first-class drug stores. Mr. Pease is also a partner with Pierre Dandurand, Jr., in a drug store at the South End, conducted under the firm name of Pease & Dandurand. Both stores are first-class pharmacies, and are conducted in a first class manner.

Mr. Pease is one of the most energetic business men, and his ambition coupled with that of other enterprising men in the north and south ends of the city, has had much to do with the business development of these sections. As will be seen by the accompanying illustration of the interior of "The Hacienda," it is one of the largest and best equipped drug stores in the city, and the stock of goods carried is as fine as can be found in any first-class pharmacy in New England. As the extreme north and south ends of the city represent the main manufacturing sections, such stores as "The Hacienda" are very much appreciated by the residents, because they are able to purchase all they need without the necessity of going to the centre of the city to trade. The neighborhood of "The Hacienda" block is destined to be an important centre, many large business establishments having already been opened here.

PEASE'S PRESCRIPTION PHARMACY — "THE HACIENDA,"
Acushnet Avenue, North End.

VIII.

The City of To-day--Points of Interest--Public Improvements.

New Bedford is seated on the western shore of the Acushnet River, a tidal inlet from Buzzard's Bay. The populous portion is about four miles in length by from three-quarters to a mile wide, and this territory slopes gently to the water, so that the place has an excellent natural drainage. The streets in general run north and south, and east and west, at right angles to each other. The lower streets near the wharves, in the central part, are devoted to manufacturing and shipping; the retail trade and the active business life is located chiefly on Purchase, Pleasant, Union and William streets, about the geo-

acres each, and are both now occupied by manufacturing and shipping establishments. Above the bridge and islands is an upper harbor of almost as great an extent as the main harbor, with which it is connected by a narrow channel between the shores of New Bedford and Fish Island.

While perhaps the Hon. W. W. Crapo in his centennial oration in 1876, somewhat overshot the mark when he said that "this bay is as charming as the Bay of Naples," and that the "physical condition and position" of the city were "delightful beyond comparison," yet he is so far justified that there are days in perfect weather when this opinion is almost wholly correct in essentials. A view of the harbor from one of the wharves, or from the old drawbridge in the early hours of a bright summer morning, with the

CUSTOM HOUSE AND POST OFFICE, WILLIAM STREET.

graphical centre of the populous part of the city; the side streets, and those on the upper part, and on the top of the ridge, are occupied by the homes of the people; and the cotton manufacturing districts, with their huge mills, their tenement houses, and their own local business, are located at the north and south ends respectively.

In front of the city the Acushnet River forms a fine harbor, about three-quarters of a mile wide by a mile long, with the wharves of New Bedford on the west side, and those of Fairhaven on the east, while the entrance from Buzzard's Bay is protected by Palmer's Island, which serves as a natural breakwater. The northern limit of the harbor is the New Bedford and Fairhaven bridge, about 4,000 feet long, which spans the river in three separate sections, uniting Fish Island by a drawbridge with New Bedford, next forming a link between Fish and Pope's Island, and then connecting the latter with the Fairhaven shore. These two islands are small, of a few

10-W

shipping in the harbor to give life to the scene, and the shores of Fairhaven and Sconticut Neck affording a picturesque background, presents a most charming picture. The view of the bay from the heights of Mount Pleasant is also very beautiful. From Fairhaven, from Fort Phenix, or from Palmer's Island the city presents a fine appearance, with its fine water front, the old whalers in the foreground, the sailboats, yachts, schooners, ships, steamers, and tugs at anchor, at the wharves, or moving over the waters of the harbor; the spires of the churches and the roofs of the houses rising above the tree tops; the whole city, on account of its situation on a slope lying parallel to the water, spread out to the view of the spectator.

In respect to maritime advantages the city is well situated. Along the harbor front are thirty-two substantial wharves. The harbor has been deepened at various times by the National Government, at a total expense up to 1896 of $82,694.37. As a result of these operations a channel 18 feet deep and 200 feet wide has been dredged from the deep waters of the bay below Palmer's Island to the city's wharves. An extensive anchorage area of an average depth of 15 feet at mean low water exists in the centre of the harbor.

Excellent transportation facilities are furnished by the Old Colony Railroad. The New Bedford and

A fine system of electric street railways traverse the city in all directions and reach all the important suburbs. The first street railway was put in operation in 1872 by the New Bedford and Fairhaven Street Railway Company. In 1885 the Acushnet Street Railway Company was organized, and built tracks all through the city to compete with the older company.

BROOKLAWN PARK.

BROOKLAWN PARK.

THE COMMON

SUTTONWOOD PARK.

BROOKLAWN PARK.

Taunton Railroad was opened for travel July 1, 1840, was extended to tide water in 1873-4, was consolidated with the Boston, Clinton and Fitchburg Railroad at the same time, and on Jan. 1, 1879, became part of the Old Colony system. The railroad to Fall River was built in 1875-6. The railroad station is at the North End, on the shore of the upper harbor at the foot of Pearl street; but trains during the summer run a mile further, to the steamboat wharf, to make connections for Martha's Vineyard and Nantucket.

Early in 1887 the two companies were consolidated under the name of Union Street Railway Co.

A public water supply, obtained by constructing a dam across the valley of the Acushnet brook, seven miles north of the city, was first put in operation in 1869. An additional supply, for use during the dry season, was in 1886 secured by tapping Little Quittacas Pond, two miles north of the storage reservoir. As a result of the great increase in manufacturing and of the growth of the population after 1880, these sources of supply were taxed to their full capacity.

and the necessity of a better system became every year more apparent. After much negotiation and agitation, an act was finally passed in 1894 by the state legislature, authorizing the city to use the water of the Great and Little Quittacas ponds in Middleboro, and the city council, on Nov. 8, 1894, appropriated $1,200,000 to carry out the project. This undertaking is now nearly completed, and will put New Bedford in possession of a water system sufficient for a city of twice its present size. The water of the ponds will be forced "through a gradually rising steel pipe eight miles long, to the large distributing reservoir located upon the highest point of land to be found within a practical distance from New Bedford — a point called High Hill in Dartmouth."

The original supply is very dark in color, owing to the fact that it is largely drained from extensive swamps; but according to an analysis made by Prof. William R. Nichols, in 1885, it is wholesome for drinking and domestic uses. The new water, however, will be received direct from the ponds. It is exceptionally fine in quality and clear in color, and forms a marked contrast to the "amber colored fluid" the citizens are now obliged to use.

The New Bedford and Fairhaven bridge was originally built in 1796, was washed away in 1807,

HON. WILLIAM W. CRAPO.

rebuilt soon after, and again destroyed in the September gale of 1815. It was not again rebuilt until 1819, and then endured until its destruction by the September gale of 1869. The franchise of the bridge corporation was then purchased, and a new bridge erected, which was finished in 1870, and opened as a free bridge. The latter structure has endured to the present, but is now being replaced by a strong and costly structure, 70 feet wide, the estimated cost of which is about $400,000. The section between Fairhaven and Pope's Island is now about completed. The railroad grade crossing at the New Bedford end will probably be abolished, but whether by elevating the railroad or the roadway, has not, as yet, been decided. The elevation of the bridge and roadway would be far the best solution, as topographical con-

ditions favor that plan, while to elevate the railroad would require the erection of an unsightly trestle at an enormous expense. The drawbridge will be relocated and widened.

New Bedford has recently developed an excellent system of public parks. The Common, on Purchase street, just west of the railroad, was until a few years ago the only public ground, and it was for a long time what the name implied, a playground for the children, a ball ground for the boys, and the scene of public celebrations. Many improvements have been made since 1890. The Common is no longer what it was, but is a beautiful and well-cared-for little park, with more of the character of a public garden than an old-time town green. Brooklawn Park, formerly the estate of Daniel Ricketson, the first historian of the city, is located on Acushnet avenue, north of the populous portion of the city, and is a very attractive locality. Buttonwood Park, on Kempton street, to the westward of the city, has within its limits a large pond, which is popular for skating. Marine Park is in the immediate neighborhood of Fort Taber at Clark's Point, the southern and seaward end of the city, and can be reached either by the Point road, around Clark's Point peninsula, or by the Middle Point ave. across the peninsula. Since 1890 about $150,000 have been spent on these parks.

A number of fine public buildings adorn the city, chief among which are the Public Library; the City Hall, surrounded by a little park, corner of Pleasant and William streets; the Custom House, at corner of William and North Second streets, erected in 1836; the Bristol County Court House, on County street, erected in 1831; the Jail and House of Correction, on Court and Union streets. The first jail was erected in 1829. New Bedford became one of the shire towns of Bristol County in 1828. The new Post Office building, corner of William street and Acushnet avenue, was completed in 1895. Since 1890 many fine business blocks have been erected in the central part of the city, and the principal structures are: Odd Fellows Building, corner of Pleasant and William streets; Masonic Building, corner

MAYOR CHARLES S. ASHLEY.

Union and Pleasant streets; Merchants Bank Building, corner Purchase and William streets; Standard Building, Market street, opposite City Hall; Five Cents Savings Bank Building, 37 Purchase street; and the building of the New Bedford Institution for Savings, corner Union and Fourth streets. These are all beautiful structures, in recent styles of architecture, and add greatly to the appearance of the central section of the city.

The wealthy whaling merchants erected large mansions on County street in the early and middle years of the century. In reference to these George F. Tucker remarks: "Many of them are unfortunate in their architectural finish, as their proud but unlettered builders enjoined the imitation of the Grecian or Roman temple. But who will deny they are imposing, and where will you find in the old commercial cities of New England other residences with such abundant surroundings of garden and lawn?" On County street and adjacent avenues are many modern type houses which contrast oddly with these older dwellings.

Two daily papers are published in the city — the *Mercury* established by Benjamin Lindsey as a weekly in 1807, and as a daily in 1841, and the *Standard*, started in 1850 by Edmund Anthony, and still conducted by his sons Edmund and Benjamin Anthony. The former is a morning and the latter an evening paper. The most prominent and able journalist in the city is William L. Sayer, who was editor of the *Mercury* from 1876 until 1893, during which period he gave the paper a high standing as an independent journal. Since 1893 Mr. Sayer has edited the *Standard*. Zephaniah W. Pease, the present collector of the port, is now editor of the *Mercury*. He is a fluent and graceful writer and a man of scholarly tastes. William G. Kirschbaum, reporter on the *Standard* and correspondent of the *Boston Herald*, is a painstaking and hustling newsgatherer. Among the younger journalists deserving of mention, are George A.

Hough, city editor of the *Standard*, William M. Emery, night editor of the *Mercury*, and Harry W. Butler, reporter on the *Standard*. The business of both papers is conducted by Geo. S. Fox. A French daily paper, *L'Echo Du Soir*, is now published at 760 Purchase Street, and the editor and manager is J. A. Caron. *The Whaleman's Shipping List*, a weekly paper which contains complete lists of the whaleships, where they are, their catch in oil and bone, etc., in tabulated form, was established by Henry Lindsey in 1843, was owned by Benjamin Lindsey from 1853 to 1875, when it came into the possession of E. P. Raymond, who had managed it from 1861. Mr. Raymond conducted it until his death in 1889, since which time it has been issued as a single sheet by George R. Phillips.

In addition to its other advantages as a manufacturing locality, the rate of taxation has been greatly reduced in New Bedford since 1893. This was mainly the result of the persistence and courage of one of the assessors, George E. Briggs, who was instrumental in raising the assessment on large areas of vacant land, which had risen greatly in value because of the proximity of the new factories and new houses that were erected during the booms in 1888 and 1892. As in other cities, the large and wealthy estates were taxed lightly, and the people owning large areas were assessed on a low valuation, while small owners, and single lots were taxed at a high figure. Mr. Briggs endeavored to change this condition of affairs in order to secure greater justice to all, and succeeded at least in a measure, although he met with much opposition and made many enemies. The statistics show what was accomplished. In 1893 the valuation was $41,175,095, the rate of taxation $17.50, and the amount raised $801,290. The next year, when the new plan came into operation, the valuation was $51,131,925, the rate $15.60, and the amount raised $828,541. In 1895 the valuation was $52,612,733, the rate $15.40, and the income $839,298. In 1896 the valuation was $56,281,117, the rate $15.40 and the income $897,679. The rate in 1897 was $16.20.

Although New Bedford has not realized an ideal condition in her social development, she has yet made very perceptible progress in the last twenty-five years. The struggle and contention of politics and business, while apparently at times full of evil, has in the end brought forth good, and the outlook is consequently hopeful for the future both as to the city itself and the condition of the people.

Charles S. Ashley.

The present Mayor of New Bedford, Charles S. Ashley, is a native of the city. In 1876 he engaged in the clothing and gentlemen's furnishing business at 72 78 Williams Street, and conducted it until recently at that location, the style of the firm being Ashley & Pierce. He was also interested for years, in the wholesale provision business. He has represented his fellow citizens in the Common Council and on the Board of Aldermen, and besides his present term was mayor of the city in 1891-2. He was postmaster of New Bedford from 1893 to the present year. He is a member of the I. O. O. F., the Knights of Pythias, belongs to the Wamsutta, Dartmouth and Merchant Clubs of this city and to the Mayors' Club.

SEMI-CENTENNIAL CELEBRATION.

A Brief Summary of the Inception and Progress of the Undertaking.

General Programme, List of Committees, Routes of the Processions, Industrial Exhibition and Preliminary List of Exhibitors.

The idea of a Semi-Centennial Celebration of the incorporation of the city of New Bedford, is said to have been first publicly suggested by George F. Bartlett, at a meeting of the Board of Trade in September, 1896. It was favorably received, and a committee of the Board of Trade was appointed to bring the matter before the city council. A joint special committee was appointed early the present year to make provision for a celebration, and on March 26, 1897, the council voted to appropriate $8,000 for a semi-centennial celebration provided the citizens raised $2,000 by subscription. A public meeting was held in the City Hall on the evening of June 7, when this amount was pledged, and a committee of citizens was appointed to act in concert with the Board of Aldermen and the Common Council, the whole number to form a general committee to carry out the celebration.

Notwithstanding many differences of opinion as to the advisability of holding the celebration at this time, and considerable opposition, both covert and open, from conservative citizens, the committee labored strenuously, and in the face of great discouragements and difficulties has succeeded in organizing a celebration of which the city may well be proud, and which will reflect honor not only on the members of the committee, but will be an unmistakable benefit to the community.

GENERAL COMMITTEE.

Chairman:

MAYOR CHARLES S. ASHLEY.

Vice-Chairman:

STEPHEN A. BROWNELL, (Ex-Mayor).
Secretary: Z. W. PEASE, (Collector of the Port).
Treasurer: JAMES H. HATHAWAY, (City Treasurer).

Aldermen:

HENRY P. JENNEY,   HENRY C. DENISON,
GEORGE A. HOUGH,   MANUEL V. SYLVIA,
SAMUEL C. HUNT,   SAMUEL E. BENTLEY.

Councilmen:

Ernest Findeisen,   Frank A. Habicht,
Stephen L. Finnel,   Chas. H. Fuller,
Frederick L. Dawe,   John A. Taylor,
Joseph Magnant,   Robert L. Baylies,
Arthur L. Blackmer,   Clifton H. Cornish,
William Bamford,   Joseph Dias,
George P. Bailey,   Philip C. Russell,
William L. Chadwick,   George N. Gardiner,
Oliver B. Davis,   Edward F. Penney,
Walter A. Jenney,   William J. Bullock,
Clifton W. Bartlett,   Joseph C. Warren.

Citizens:

Abbott P. Smith,   David L. Parker,
Martin P. Fichtenmayer, Daniel G. Dinnigan,
George E. Briggs,   John Duff,
Joseph Poisson,   John McCullough,
Benjamin H. Anthony,   Wm. T. Taylor,
Henry S. Hutchinson,   Ralph T. Callowhill,
Rev. James F. Clark,   Dr. A. F. Wyman,
Joseph Dawson,   W. H. B. Remington,
J. Arthur Taylor,   Harry W. Butler,
Chas. F. Shaw,   George F. Bartlett,
Geo. R. Stetson,   Rufus A. Soule,
Robert F. Raymond,   Edward J. A. Zeiner,
Geo. B. Richmond,   Hoyland Smith,
James N. Parker,   W. E. Hatch,
E. E. Rewick,   Nathan C. Hathaway,
Geo. S. Fox,   Edmund Anthony, Jr.
E. C. Brownell,   Thomas H. Knowles,
A. J. Alley, Jr.,   Clement N. Swift,
Albion T. Brownell,   George H. Nye,
C. H. Gifford.   Fred D. Stanley,
J. C. Patnaude,   L. Z. Normandin,
Edward M. Peirce,   William F. Williams,

Sub-Committees.

Committee on Program Clifton W. Bartlett, Henry S. Hutchinson, A. P. Smith, Dr. M. V. Silvia, Rev. Fr. James F. Clark.

Committee on Industrial Exhibition—Geo. E. Briggs, Abbott P. Smith, Henry C. Denison, Clifton H. Cornish, Edward F. Penney.

Executive Committee—George R. Stetson, Stephen L. Finnell, Benjamin H. Anthony, Frank A. Habicht, George E. Briggs.

Committee on Gathering of Old Residents George B. Richmond, Charles F. Shaw.

Committee on Special Church Services Robert F. Raymond, Rev. Fr. James F. Clark, Samuel C. Hunt, Joseph Poisson, Oliver B. Davis.

Committee on Trades Procession E. E. Rewick, Henry S. Hutchinson, Samuel C. Hunt, Edward F. Penney, James N. Parker, Edward M. Pierce.

Committee on Military and Civic Parade—Dr. M. V. Sylvia, George E. Briggs, J. Arthur Taylor, George N. Gardiner, Stephen L. Finnell, George S. Fox, William F. Williams.

Committee on Invitations and Receptions—The Chairman, Vice-Chairman, and Secretary, and Chairmen of all Sub-Committees.

Committee on Publicity and Promotion George A. Hough, Benjamin H. Anthony, S. A. Brownell, Dr. M. V. Sylvia.

Committee on Museum A. P. Smith, Nathan C. Hathaway, Edmund Anthony, Jr., Thos. H. Knowles, Clement N. Swift.

Committee on Bicycle Parade—J. Arthur Taylor, Dr. A. F. Wyman, Walter S. Jenney, Ralph T. Callowhill, William Bamford, Hoyland Smith, Geo. H. Nye, Fred D. Stanley.

Committee on Athletic Sports Dr. M. V. Sylvia, William J. Bullock, Clifton W. Bartlett, D. G. Dinnigan, Joseph Dias, Philip C. Russell.

Committee on Music Abbott P. Smith, John Taylor, Thomas J. Gifford, E. J. A. Zeiner, S. C. Hunt.

Committee on Transportation Rufus A. Soule, Fred D. Stanley, Charles F. Shaw.

Committee on Literary Exercises—Robert T. Raymond, Rev. Fr. James F. Clark, David L. Parker, William T. Taylor, William E. Hatch.

Committee on Badges—Joseph Dias, E. C. Brownell, Arthur L. Blackmer, Charles H. Fuller, E. E. Rewick, Frank A. Habicht.

Committee on Printing and Advertising Clifton W. Bartlett, Henry S. Hutchinson, James N. Parker, Benjamin H. Anthony, Robert L. Baylies.

Committee on Properties—Samuel C. Hunt, George E. Briggs, Martin P. Fichtenmayer, Henry S. Hutchinson, E. E. Rewick.

Committee on Illuminations and Decorations—Daniel G. Dinnigan, William T. Taylor, Ernest Findeisen, James N. Parker, J. Arthur Taylor.

Committee on Banquet— Rev. Fr. James F. Clark, Samuel C. Hunt, Abbott P. Smith, Robert F. Raymond, Thomas J. Gifford.

PROGRAMME OF THE CELEBRATION.

Sunday, October 10, 1897.

10:30 A. M.　Services in the different churches.

2:30 P. M　Service of song in tent on Union Street. Singing by the Semi-Centennial Chorus accompanied by band.

Monday, October 11, 1897

Three salutes fired by the U. S. S. Amphitrite.

9:00 A. M.　Opening of Industrial Exhibition. Music. speeches by Hon. W. W. Crapo and others.

10:00 to 10:30 A. M.　Concert by the Semi-Centennial Band in tent on Union Street,

10:30 A. M.　Literary Exercises in the tent on Union St. Oration by George Fox Tucker.

2:00 P. M.　Handicap Bicycle Road Race on the Point Road. 20 miles, 22 prizes.

3:00 P. M.　Drill and Concert by U. S. Artillery and Band from Fort Adams, at Buttonwood Park.

8:00 P. M.　Illuminated Bicycle Parade, starting from City Hall. 7 classes, 14 prizes.

Industrial Exhibition open from 9:00 A. M to 10:00 P. M. Building on Weld Street.

U. S. S. Amphitrite open for Inspection daily.

Tuesday, October 12, 1897.

GOVERNOR'S DAY.

10:30 A. M.　Governor's salute of seventeen guns to be fired by the U. S. S. Amphitrite, on arrival of Governor.

11:00 A. M.　Military and Civic Parade. starting from City Hall.

1:00 P. M.　Playout by Veteran Firemen, Park Square,

3:00 P. M.　Drill and concert by U. S. Artillery Company and Band from Fort Adams, at Buttonwood Park.

NEW BEDFORD INDUSTRIAL EXHIBITION BUILDING, WELD STREET.—NORTH END.

3:30 P. M.　Review of First Regiment at Buttonwood Park.

4:00 P. M　Dress Review of First Regiment at Buttonwood Park.

8:00 P. M.　Dinner. Hon. H. M. Knowlton, toastmaster.

Industrial Exhibition open from 10:00 A. M. to 10:00 P. M., Building on Weld Street.

Three salutes fired by U. S. S. Amphitrite.

U. S. S. Amphitrite open for Inspection daily.

Wednesday, October 13, 1897.

MERCHANT'S DAY.

10:30 A. M.　Trades Procession and Horse Parade. starting from City Hall.

3:00 P. M.　Drill and concert by U. S. Artillery Company and Band from Fort Adams, at Buttonwood Park.

Industrial Exhibition open from 10:00 A. M. to 10:00 P.M.

Three salutes fired by U. S. S. Amphitrite.

U. S. S. Amphitrite open for inspection daily.

Thursday, October 14, 1897.

10:30 A. M.   Literary and Musical Exercises in the tent on Union Street, arranged especially for school children.

1:00 P. M.   Whaleboat race on the river near East French Avenue, 3 prizes.

2:00 P. M.   Cutter race on the river near East French Avenue, between crews of Naval Companies from Newport, Fall River and New Bedford. Two prizes.

3:00 P. M.   Drill and concert U. S. Artillery Company, and Band from Fort Adams, at Buttonwood Park.

Industrial Exhibition open from 10:00 A. M. to 10:00 P. M., Building on Weld Street.

Three salutes fired by U. S. S. Amphitrite.

U. S. S. Amphitrite open for inspection daily.

Friday and Saturday, October 15, and 16, 1897.

Industrial Exhibition at building on Weld Street, open from 10:00 A. M. to 10:00 P. M. Music by band each evening.

ROUTES OF THE PROCESSIONS.

Bicycle Lantern Parade, Monday Oct. 11, at 8 p. m.

F. D. Stanley, Chief Marshal.

Formation on Pleasant street, Pleasant and Weld streets, Acushnet avenue, Sawyer, New County, Linden, County, Hillman, Cottage and Court streets, Rotch avenue, Hawthorn, Cottage, Dartmouth, Rockland, County and Cove streets,West French avenue ; countermarch, Cove, County, Sixth, Russell and Fifth streets to City Hall.

Military and Civic Parade,Tuesday Oct. 12, at 11 a.m.

City Hall, Pleasant, Fifth, Grinnell, County, Linden, Pleasant, Weld, Purchase, Maxfield and Pleasant streets, and pass in review at the Library building.

Trades Procession, Wednesday Oct. 13, at 10.30 a. m.

Hon. Stephen A. Brownell, Chief Marshal.

Pleasant, Fifth and Wing streets, Acushnet avenue, Rivet, County, Linden, Pleasant, Weld, Purchase, William and Pleasant streets.

BICYCLE RACES AND PARADE.

Prizes for Bicycle Events at the Semi-Centennial Celebration, Monday, October 11.

The principal events will be a road race on the noted Point road course and an illuminated parade. The prizes offered are:

Class A. Club parading largest number of illuminated wheels, 1st prize—Roll top desk, value $35; 2d prize—Morris chair, value $20.

Class B. Club of not less than 15 uniformed members making finest display. 1st prize Couch, value $15; 2d prize Picture, value $10.

Class C. Finest illuminated gentlemen's single wheel, 1st prize—Sideboard, value $18; 2d prize—Picture, value $12.50.

Class D. Finest illuminated lady's single wheel. 1st prize—Solid silver brush and comb, value $6; 2d prize—Lady's Christy saddle, value $5.

Class E. Finest costumed rider, decoration of wheel considered, lady or gentlemen. 1st prize Marble clock, value $10; 2d prize Pair "Meteor" tires, value $7.

Class F. Finest decorated tandem. 1st prizes—Two pictures, value $7.50 each $15; 2d prizes—Two card cases, value $2.50 each $5.

Class G. For L. A. W. members only, finest L. A. W. decoration. 1st prize—Solid gold L. A. W. badge white plate, $7; 2d prize L. A. W. pin, $3.

The prizes for the 20 5-8 miles handicap road race are as follows:

1st time prize—Diamond, value $40; 2d time prize—Gold watch, value $30.

1st prizes Gold watch, $50; 2d prize—China fish service, $25; 3d prize—Shot gun, $22.50; 4th prize—Solid oak chamber set, $20; 5th prize—Suit clothes, (M. C. Swift & Sons), $15; 6th prize—French lamp, Dresden china, $12; 7th prize—Bicycle suit, $10; 8th prize—Marble clock, $8; oth prize—Traveling bag, $7.50; 10th prize—Training robe, $7; 11th prize—Pair "Meteor" tires, $7; 12th prize—Bicycle lantern, $5; 13th prize —Racing saddle, $4; 14th prize—Sweater, $3.50; 15th prize— Silver card case, $3; 16th prize—Golf stocking, $1.50; 17th prize—Lampson luggage carrier, $1.50; 18th prize—Two cans "Vimold," $1; 19th prize—Cyclometer, $1; 20th prize—Golf cay, 75 cents.

INDUSTRIAL EXHIBITION.

The leading industries of the city are well represented in the building on Weld street, at the North End, the headquarters of the Exhibition. An illustration of the structure is shown on page 78. The hall and the exhibits are elaborately decorated. In the centre of the building is the band stand, raised eight feet from the floor, and underneath is a refreshment counter. The office and information bureau of the Semi-Centennial Committee is near the band stand. The following is a partial

List of Exhibitors:

Pairpoint Manufacturing Co., glass and silverware, (machinery in motion).

New Bedford Copper Co.

Morse Twist Drill and Machine Co.

Strange Forge Drill and Tool Co.

Johnson Typesetter Co., (typesetting machine in motion).

W. S. Hill Electric Co., electric appliances, (Machinery in motion).

New York Biscuit Co.

Taber Art Co., engravings and art goods, (machinery in motion).

George Kirby, Jr., paints.

Brightman Bros., paints.

George Delano's Sons, oils.

William F. Nye, oils.

George L. Brownell, carriages.

Clarence Lowell, carriages.

H. S. Hutchinson & Co., stationery, blankbooks and bindery.

Weeden Manufacturing Co., novelties.

New Bedford Reed Co., loom reeds, (machinery in motion).

Blossom Bros., planing mill.

Fowler Loom Harness Factory, (machinery in motion).

Padelford & Besse, sash-cord braiding machines.

Patrick Keane, cut glass.

A. L. Blackmer Co., cut glass.

Pope's Island Manufacturing Co., metal novelties.

Hathaway, Soule & Harrington, shoes, (machinery in motion).

Schuler Bros., shoes, (machinery in motion).

Hedge, Lewis Manufacturing Co., eyelets and buttons

T. M. Denham & Bros., shirts.

Davis & Hatch Spice Co., upland III

L. A. Littlefield, silverplating.

Thomas Hersom & Co., soaps.

Charles F. Cushing, carriages.

STORE OF LOUIS E. SHURTLEFF, 20 PURCHASE STREET.

Louis E. Shurtleff.

An old-established store, which has long been the leading one in its line in New Bedford, is the retail jewelry business now conducted by Louis E. Shurtleff, at 20 Purchase street. The store was conducted for many years by Dexter & Haskins, then by C. W. Haskins, alone, and after that by H. S. Francis, who had been a watchmaker for Dexter & Haskins 30 years. Mr. Haskins died in 1890. Mr. Francis conducted the store from 1893 to 1895, when he was succeeded by the present proprietor, Louis E. Shurtleff. He is a young man, and came to work for Mr. Haskins in 1891, as a watchmaker, and remained in that capacity with Mr. Francis, from whom he purchased the business in 1895.

The store has always carried the largest stock, enjoyed the best reputation, and has had the cream of the trade in its line in the city. The stock now consists of a general line of first-class jewelry and watches, and special lines of sterling silverware, diamonds, novelties, French and American clocks, silk umbrellas, etc. Mr. Shurtleff also keeps chafing dishes in a large variety of patterns, at very reasonable prices, and supplies the utensils necessary to go with them, namely, chafing dish spoons, alcohol flagons, etc.

Mr. Shurtleff has had fourteen years' experience in the jewelry trade. He learned the business with E. D. Tisdale & Son of Taunton, who conducted one of the best stores in the country. He has had a varied experience both as a watchmaker and salesman. For three years he was a salesman in the diamond department for A. Stowell & Co., of Boston. In his employ at present he has an unusually good watchmaker, and two of his present clerks were with Mr. Haskins. The business occupies the entire building at this location, the upper story being devoted to workrooms and the storage of surplus stock. Mr. Shurtleff aims first to supply goods of the best quality; and second to sell them as reasonably as possible.

H. S. Hutchinson & Co.

The leading book and stationery store in New Bedford is that of H. S. Hutchinson & Co., 198 to 202

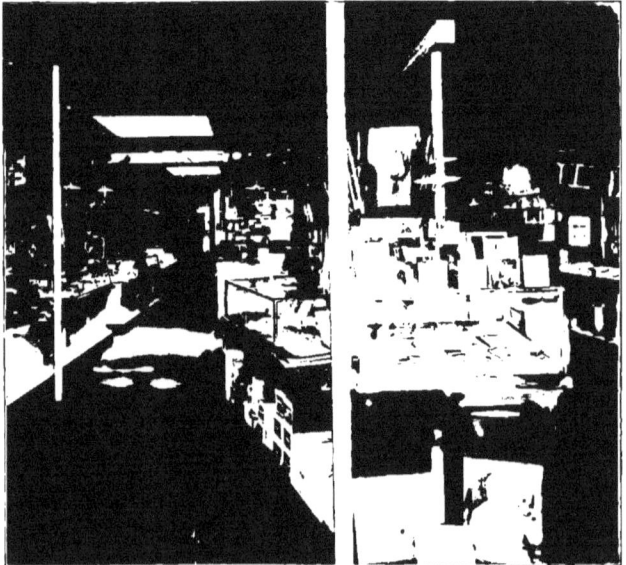

STORE OF H. S. HUTCHINSON & CO., 198 to 202 UNION STREET.

OFFICE OF THE HEDGE, LEWIS MANUFACTURING CO.,
Corner of First and Rivet Streets.

market, the book drummers say, than exists even to-day in cities of the same size. This condition has always existed, and the Hutchinsons, father and son, have catered to this demand intelligently and successfully.

The store has always carried the best and largest stock of books and stationery in the city. When it was moved into the present quarters, artists' materials, music and pictures were added, and a workshop for fitting and making picture frames was also then started in the third story and is still maintained. In 1894 a book bindery and blank book manufactory was started at 93 Union street. The present owners of the business are Mr. Hutchinson and his mother, Mrs. E. H. Hutchinson. Mr. Hutchinson was brought up in the book store, as during his school days he was constantly around on holidays and vacations. For three years he was employed in a wholesale house in the book and stationery trade in Boston, and there acquired some of the experience that has enabled him so successfully to follow in his father's footsteps.

Union street. The business was established by S. Hutchinson in 1804, and was conducted by him until his death in 1880, when his son H. S. Hutchinson succeeded to the management. From the beginning until 1875 the store was located on Cheapside, now Pleasant street, and even in those days was the leader in its line. At that time it was removed to what was then 142 Union street, now 104, where it remained until 1893, when the present commodious quarters were secured. These were formed by throwing two stores into one, making the present dimensions 34 x 99 feet, lighted at the front by two large plate glass windows.

New Bedford, no doubt owing to her Quaker ancestry, and to the large wealth that early came to her, has always had a notice able atmosphere of culture. For this reason there has been a good market for the best books a much better

Hedge, Lewis Manufacturing Company.

In the old rivet factory, a substantial stone edifice, on the corner of First and Rivet Streets, which was

11-H

THE HEDGE, LEWIS MANUFACTURING CO. —MACHINE ROOM.

C. S. JORDAN'S STUDIO, 12 PURCHASE STREET

erected about 70 years ago, the Hedge, Lewis Manufacturing Company carry on a unique industry. Here they make shoe, gaiter and upholstery buttons from papier mache by machinery specially designed for the purpose, and the arrangements in use in the shops for handling the production are extremely effective and labor saving.

This industry was started in 1888, in the premises on Acushnet Avenue, now occupied by the City Steam Laundry, by G. H. Hedge and F. H. Hardman. Fifteen months later, on account of the increased demand for the goods, larger quarters were needed and the present factory was leased. Mr. Hardman retired soon after the business was started, Mr. Albert W. Lewis then purchased an interest, and the firm became Hedge, Lewis & Co., and conducted the manufacture successfully at the new location.

Meanwhile in 1885 the firm of Hedge, Lewis & Co., in association with D. A. Corey and J. C. King started to manufacture spinning ring travelers in the upper story of the factory on Rivet Street under the name of the Reliance Manufacturing Co. Mr. King afterwards withdrew and Mr. M. A. Wood purchased his interest. In 1895 the Reliance Manufacturing Co. was consolidated with Hedge, Lewis & Co., and the consolidation took the name of the Hedge, Lewis Manufacturing Co. The increase in the demand for buttons was so great that the company found it necessary to use the entire space in the Rivet Street factory, and accordingly the ring traveler branch of the business was removed to 5 Rodman Street on September 1, 1897, where it is conducted under the name of the Reliance Manufacturing Co., and Mr. D. A. Corey is the manager. Mr. Lewis is still a member of the Hedge, Lewis Manufacturing Co., but is at present employed in the office of the Westport Manufacturing Co. Mr. G. H. Hedge the founder of the business is the treasurer and superintendent and to his practical knowledge much of the success of the industry is due. Mr. M. A. Wood is the secretary, and general salesman. At present the business is wholly under the management of Mr. Hedge and Mr. Wood.

The processes of the manufacture are extremely interesting. Three kinds of buttons are made, shoe, gaiter and upholstery, in all sizes, colors and styles. The raw material used is papier mache, which comes in sheets of about an eight of an inch in thickness. These are cut into strips which are fed into a machine that with steel dies cuts out round blanks. The latter after being rolled and hardened in a specially designed machine, are fed by a hopper into an automatic machine, which turns out the complete buttons with wire eyelets at the rate of 180 per minute. The buttons are then polished and colored by the aid of various very ingenious automatic contrivances, which renders handling almost unnecessary, and are finally finished by being baked in large ovens at a high temperature. The machinery and appliances were especially designed by Mr. Hedge and the other members of the firm, and they have been greatly improved since the origin of the business so that they produce 150 per cent. more than at first. The production is now so large that supplies of papier mache and of wire are brought in by the car load. The buttons are sold all over the United States, and a very large export trade has been developed to England, Germany, France, Austria, Italy and South America; at the Industrial Exhibition the company will make an exhibit of all stages of the product in process of manufacture and of finished buttons of all kinds.

The stone building now occupied is said to have been built by one of the Grinnell's as a rivet factory about 1830, was afterward used for various purposes, and was utilized by some of the cotton mills in the vicinity. It is 120 x 45 feet in dimensions, two stories high, and now has an ell for the engine which operates the machinery. About twenty hands are employed.

C. S. Jordan.

C. S. Jordan's photograph gallery at 12 Purchase Street, is the oldest stand in the city for this line of work, it having been established somewhere about the time of the incorporation of the city government, fifty years ago. Mr. Jordan is an artist of acknowledged ability, as his high-class productions plainly show, and his studio is well equipped with modern appliances for doing artistic work. Most of the negatives used in producing the prints for this book are in Mr. Jordan's possession, and any person desiring prints from them can secure them by applying at his place of business.

The Strange Forged Drill & Tool Co.

The twist drill was a great improvement on the old-fashioned straight machine drill, giving a better cutting edge and being easier kept in order, but its manufacture was a costly process. The groves had to be milled out of a bar of steel, the full size of the finished tool. This was a costly process both in labor and in waste of material. There were also qualities of steel so hard that they could not be milled, and though very desirable for some classes of work, for the above reasons could not be used. A veteran blacksmith conceived the idea of forging the twist in the drill instead of milling it, and after much experimenting, succeeded in making accurate "twist drills" by the new process.

After perfecting and patenting the process, he went through many tribulations as a manufacturer, and it is only quite recently that a strong company has been formed under the name of Strange Forged Drill & Tool Co., of New Bedford, Mass., and is now making all sizes of forged twist drills in large quantities. Owing to the small amount of labor required in making the forged drills as compared with the milled drills, and also the fact that there is practically no waste of metal, the new drills can be made for less money than the old style, and yet exhaustive tests would show

THE STRANGE FORGED DRILL AND TOOL CO.—FORGE ROOM.

THE STRANGE FORGED DRILL AND TOOL CO. MACHINE ROOM.

that their wearing qualities are very superior. A prominent machine manufacturing company of Indiana, reports giving the forged drills a test on some special machinery steel, three and one fourth inches in diameter and says: "The best results we had ever previously got out of any drill, was to drill two holes that would be equal to drilling through six and a half inches. Then we would have to stop and grind. With your forged drills we have drilled nine holes, or twenty-nine and one-fourth inches, without a stop to grind." The company are also now making to order drills out of the celebrated "Mushet" self-hardening steel, and claim that this is the only process by which a perfect drill can be made from this celebrated steel. So confident are the officers of the company that their drills

of building lumber, which is mostly brought here in vessels and unloaded at the wharf of the Wamsutta Mills, foot of Wamsutta street. Spruce and hemlock timber and shingles are received from Down East, by vessels; clapboards and pine from West Virginia and other parts of the South by cars. The lumber has been mostly sold in the vicinity to the builders and contractors who have done so much construction during the past few years in this part of the city at the time of the booms resulting from the erection of the cotton mills. From six to fifteen men are employed in and about the lumber yard. The members of the firm are Elias Terry, and his son K. Clifton Terry.

Fournier & Nicholson.

Among the leading industrial establishments at the North End of New Bedford at present is the plan-

E. & K. C. TERRY'S LUMBER YARDS, AND FOURNIER & NICHOLSON'S PLANING MILL, BOWDITCH STREET.

will do all that is claimed for them, that they are willing to send a sample to all responsible manufacturers who will undertake to give them a fair test. The company are also making a new and improved chuck that is very much liked by all who have used it.

E. & K. C. Terry.

Between Bowditch street and the railroad tracks at the North End of the city, is the extensive lumber yards of E. & K. C. Terry. The office of the firm is at 27 to 29 Bowditch street. The premises comprise an area of about two acres, on which are five lumber sheds of the following dimensions: one 185 x 20 feet; two each 60 x 20 feet and two each 200 x 50 feet. The business was established at this location in 1892, by the present firm, the members of which had, however, had considerable experience in this line elsewhere. The firm carries a large general assortment

ing mill of Fournier & Nicholson, at 31 to 35 Bowditch street. The business was established at this location in 1802 by the present firm. The original mill was 40 x 125 feet in dimensions, but an addition of 25 x 60 feet was built in 1894. About one hundred and fifty feet north of the mill are two store-houses, one 26 x 40 feet, and two stories in height, and the other 24 x 36 feet, three stories in height. The mill is provided with all modern machinery and conveniences, and doors, sashes and blinds are manufactured in large quantities, while window frames, mouldings and brackets are also turned out. All kinds of work is done to order in planing, turning and circular sawing. In the storehouse about 1,600 doors, 1,000 windows of sash and 1,000 pairs blinds are kept on hand constantly in stock sizes, so that the demands of builders can be supplied readily and quickly.

INTERIOR FOURNIER & NICHOLSON'S PLANING MILL.

About fifteen men, all skilled workmen, are constantly employed. The members of the firm are E. Fournier and J. G. Nicholson. Mr. Fournier has had many years' practical experience in this industry, and he is the superintendent of the planing mill, for which his skill and mechanical ability amply fits him. Mr. Nicholson is the financial manager and the salesman, and conducts the office business. To his acumen much of the success of the enterprise is due. The firm started practically without capital, but has been very prosperous, and now is on an exceptionally good financial foundation.

Bradford D. Tripp.

Progress in industry is accomplished not only by the invention of new machinery but by the application of new methods to old conditions. Mr. Bradford D. Tripp has succeeded in an endeavor of the latter kind at his shop 92 Pleasant street, New Bedford, where he has adjusted the machinery of the modern shoe factory to the task of repairing shoes. This seems at first sight a very simple thing, but it has never been done before. Mr. Tripp is the pioneer and its success will revolutionize shoe repairing.

Mr. Tripp started his present shop Feb. 15, 1897. The idea occurred to him several years ago when working in the Brockton shoe factories where he was engaged several years. Although his shop has only been in operation a few months it is the best equipped repair shop in the country, and the only one that accomplishes the work by machinery. The machines used are stitchers, sewers, nailers and finishers, the same as are used in shoe factories. Mr. Tripp's plant has a capacity of turning out twelve pairs of new shoes daily, but 40 pairs can be repaired with the present force of employees, although the capacity in repairing is practically unlimited.

The following quotation from the *Boot and Shoe Recorder* of June 23, 1897, shows that the reasonableness of Mr. Tripp's method is recognized by experts, but he had put the idea into effect before this opinion was written:

"It is only a matter of time before machinery can by power will be introduced to shoe repairing. A it has been proven that the mending gives to the shoe shop a more and more everyday, and ideas that if the stores who together employ 8 or 10 men, called the work to one man, he could amount to a man shop with power and machinery. The work could then be so divided there as to make each work man an expert in these branches. The public would get better work for the same money, and the stores would make more money and less trouble than they have now with their men cramped up in some corner without the least facilities for their work, shelf worn goods could be fixed up better and it would be an improvement all round."

Mr. Tripp has found that he can do an independent business at least at present, much better than by working for the stores, and he has developed an excellent trade, which is constantly increasing in amount.

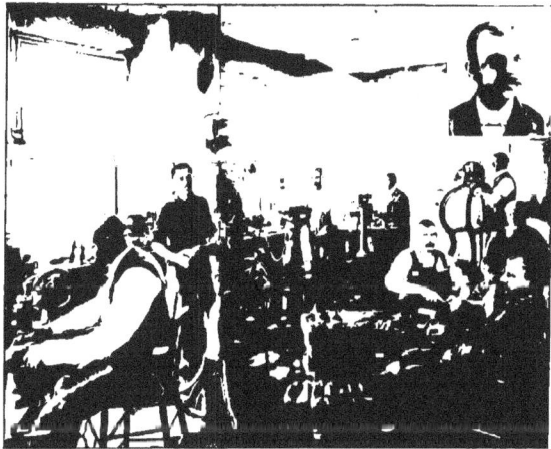

BRADFORD D. TRIPP'S SHOE REPAIR SHOP, 92 PLEASANT STREET.

Benjamin Dawson & Son.

In 1868, when New Bedford was just about entering upon her career as a manufacturing city, and all the cotton manufacture in its limits was carried on in the three stone mills of the Wamsutta Corporation, Benjamin Dawson started a small grocery store on the southeast corner of Purchase and Merrimac streets. He understood the wants of the people in his vicinity. As new mills were built he gradually increased his business and in the course of time accumulated considerable property. In 1880 he erected a three story brick building, corner of Purchase and Hazard streets, into which he removed his grocery store.

Two years later he transformed his business, and

concern imports the finest brands of wines, brandies, ales and stout from the old world, among which are: G. H. Munm & Co.'s Champagnes, Duff Gordon Sherries, Cossart Gorden Madeiras, Morgan & Offley's Ports; Hennessey, Martell & Co.'s, Otard Depuy & Co.'s and Bisquit Dubouché & Co.'s brandies; Bass & Co.'s and S. Allsop & Sons' English Ales from Burton-on-Trent; and Guinness' Dublin Stout. The firm supplies the first-class family and local trade of the city, with both domestic and foreign liquors.

The senior partner Benjamin Dawson for many years took a very active part in politics. He was a member of the common council four years, served two years in the board of alderman, and for one year was

HEADQUARTERS OF BENJAMIN DAWSON & SON,
Importers of Whole-de Wine and Spirit Merchants,   Cor. Purchase and Hazard Streets, New Bedford

became an importer and wholesale wine and spirit merchant. Success crowned his efforts, and he has been one of the chief dealers in this line in the city. In the early part of the present year his son Joseph was admitted to a partnership, and the business is now conducted under the style of Benjamin Dawson & Son.

The firm occupies the lower floor of the building corner Hazard and Purchase Streets. It is agent for Frank Jones Brewing Co., N. H., fine golden and cream ales; Bowler Bros., Worcester, Mass., sparkling and matchless ales and porter; Bartholomay Brewing Co., Rochester, N. Y., fine beers; J. H. Cutter's Whiskeys; W. A. Gaines & Co., Kentucky Old Hermitage Rye and Old Crow Bourbon, and also receives all the fine Kentucky Bourbons and Maryland Rye Whiskies.

Besides this line of leading domestic products the

overseer of the poor. He has always been a Democrat. Joseph Dawson was also a city councilman for four years, and the last year of his service was president of the body, when by virtue of his position he was ex-officio a member of the board of public works and of all the principal committees.

Tichon & Foster.

Tichon & Foster, machinists, 8 Seneca street, have developed a fine business as steam engine and mill repairers. The members of the firm, Joseph E. Tichon and Henry S. Foster, are practical mechanics. By attending directly to their own work, and hustling around among the mills they have secured numerous orders, and now have work for half a dozen men. Particular attention is paid to the repairing of steel rolls, flyers, pressers and bolsters, shafting, hangers and pulleys, and all kinds of loom cranks. New machinery has recently been added

ALLEN SMITH, JR., LIVERY, HACK AND BOARDING STABLE, 38 BEDFORD St.

Allen Smith, Jr.

One of the oldest livery, hack and boarding stables in the city of New Bedford at the present time is that conducted by Allen Smith, Jr., at 38 Bedford Street. The business was established about 40 years ago by Harvey Sherman, and Samuel Bliss, who conducted it under the firm name of Sherman & Bliss.

Mr. Sherman eventually sold out and Mr. Bliss then conducted it alone. He was followed by Anthony & Lapham, who were succeeded by Cornell & Lapham, J. L. Ashley, and Eugene Hayden. Allen Smith, Jr., entered the business as an associate of Mr. Hayden, and they formed the firm of Hayden & Smith. In 1892 Mr. Hayden retired, and since then Mr. Smith has conducted the stable under his own name. The stable is large and well appointed, and has accommodations for thirty-five horses. The best trade is catered to and secured. The stable is open day and night. A specialty is made of furnishing hacks for funerals, weddings, christenings and private parties, and they are always kept in first-class condition. All the hacks now in use are new. Special attention is given to catering for the trade of transient visitors to the city, and any of the out-of-town people who are here to see the celebration can secure a carriage in short order by telephoning to Mr. Smith- his number is 357 3 and orders so received are promptly filled. Many horses are boarded at the stable. Their owners can be certain from past experience that the equines will always receive the best of care.

S. T. Rex.

On Dartmouth Street, opposite the Rural Cemetery, S T Rex carries on a general monumental business, cutting, marble and granite headstones and mortuary monuments and all kinds of cemetery work. He employs on an average about half a dozen men. Mr. Rex is himself a very expert stone cutter. He learned his trade 23 years ago at the Rhode Island Granite Works, Westerly, R. I. where he worked for seven or eight years. He then worked two years and a half for Charles P. Chapman, Westerly, and after that spent a year at Groton, Conn., in the same business. From there he went to Quincy, Mass., where he lived for ten years, working as a journeyman at his trade part of the time, but for three years he had charge of E. C. Williston's granite yard, with an oversight over a force of from fifty to eighty men. For one year also he was in business for himself in Quincy.

He came to New Bedford in April 1869 and bought out the stone yard he now conducts from Swithin Brothers, of Quincy, who conducted it as a branch business. He has conducted the business successfully. He does work for all the cemeteries in New Bedford and has carried monuments and stones to Boston, Providence and Worcester. He is the only thoroughly experienced and practical man in the working of granite in the city.

S. T. REX, MONUMENTAL WORKS, DARTMOUTH STREET.

BEST ⎰Material ⎱Workmanship ⎰Results

ARE WHAT HAVE MADE THE

Cotton Machinery
OF THE
A. T. Atherton Machine Co.
THE MOST POPULAR
AND EXTENSIVELY USED TO-DAY.

Estimates Cheerfully Given on New Plans, or Remodeling
Old Ones.

PAWTUCKET. R. I.

PROVIDENCE BELTING COMPANY

MANUFACTURERS OF

Pure Oak-Tanned Leather Belting

—— AND ——

Folded Twist Round Belting.

Our HIGH-GRADE LEATHER for Covering Worsted Rolls is considered by all to be the BEST manufactured.

OFFICE AND WORKS: **37-39 CHARLES STREET,**

PROVIDENCE, R. I.

——THE——

JOURNAL OF COMMERCE CO.

(INCORPORATED)

PROVIDENCE, R. I.

❊ ❊ ❊

Printers and Publishers

of this SOUVENIR BOOK.

❊ ❊ ❊